AF869184

AMERICA'S LAW FIRM

Built to Win: Bound to Fail

Cordell Parvin

Copyright © 2026 by
Cordell Parvin

ALL RIGHTS RESERVED. No part of this book may be reproduced or transmitted in any form by any means, electronic or mechanical, including photocopying and recording, or by any information storage and retrieval system, except as may be expressly permitted in writing from the author.

Hardcover ISBN: 978-1-971045-05-4
Paperback ISBN: 978-1-971045-06-1

Published by:
Pine Book Writing
www.PineBookWriting.com
R-10225 Yonge St Suite #250, Richmond Hill, ON L4C 3B2, Canada.

Printed in the United States of America

This is a work of fiction. Names, characters, businesses, organizations, places, events, and incidents are either the products of the author's imagination or used in a fictitious manner. Any resemblance to actual persons, living or dead, or actual events or locales is entirely coincidental. The situations and characters in this book are purely fictional, and are not intended to represent specific law firms, legal professionals, or real-life events.

Chapter 1
The Question

#

There was a time when college athletes stayed at one school, driven by loyalty and the chance to earn a degree. They stayed because that was what you did. You earned your spot, you worked hard, and you finished what you started. That changed with the arrival of Name, Image, and Likeness. NIL, they call it. Now, athletes bounce from school to school, chasing bigger paydays and better exposure. Some say it has forever altered, maybe even ruined, college sports.

Law was no different. There was a time when lawyers joined a firm and stayed, driven by loyalty and the hope of partnership. You built relationships. You helped each other rise. Once profits per partner became the only metric that mattered and those numbers were made public, everything shifted. Loyalty meant nothing if your numbers did not meet expectations. The profession became a business, and business was brutal.

That shift did not come overnight, but when it did, it left no one in the profession untouched.

This is the story of a law firm that rose by pushing for more money, more clients, and more growth, and fell because of it.

#

The summer heat isn't a problem on the top floor of the Lambert Building. Texas is air-conditioned from the neck up, so I'm not surprised. I'm twenty minutes early, which means I'm not late, and I don't have to dry my shirt.

The lobby looks like classic Dallas, modernized to reassure clients who expect results. I never thought I'd set foot in a big firm's lobby again.

Twenty years ago, Mike Carson and I left a large Dallas firm to start Carlisle and Carson, vowing to avoid places like this. We built it into a twenty-lawyer operation. It worked until it didn't.

Mike ran the finances. I trusted him. Then Tessa walked in one day with a spreadsheet she wasn't supposed to see. What it revealed ended that trust for good.

"You need to look at this," she had said, and closed the door.

My bonus that never showed up was only the beginning. Tessa had found Mike's quiet transfers, his padded reimbursements, and the line items that didn't make sense. When I pushed, the truth came fast. Mike had been skimming. He'd taken enough to wreck us both if I made it public.

I didn't make it public. I let him go quietly. Then I decided to do the same.

Which brought me here.

Cassidy Knox, one of the firm's top litigators, shakes my hand like she knows why I'm here. Her handshake is brief, her expression flat. Everything about her says she came prepared and expects the same from me. Her eyes scan quickly, as if sizing me up, calculating whether I meet their high standards for lateral partners.

I had read about Cassidy online before the interview. DFW Magazine had named her a Rising Star, the firm's youngest partner to land a Fortune 500 client. Her photo showed someone polished and composed, eyes sharp and watchful, aware of the camera rather than performing for it. I wondered whether she would live up to the billing or whether it was the usual gloss firms pay for and call recognition.

She leads me toward the conference room, setting the pace without looking back. The conference room could house a Dallas football fan's tailgate party, with room to spare. It feels airier with only Cassidy, Charles McAllister, and me.

I sit in a chair that must have cost more than my first year of undergrad. It's engineered to make me feel comfortable, but it doesn't.

Cassidy takes her seat without ceremony. When she stares without speaking, I wonder what she's thinking.

Charles McAllister, the firm's longtime managing partner, stays easy in his chair. His Rolex catches the light as he steeples his fingers. He doesn't need to speak often. Being in the room signals control. He's the kind of guy who likes being the one who decides who joins the firm, who makes partner, and how much money each partner will make. He gets right to the point. "How much business did you bring in last year?"

"Two and a half million."

McAllister's lips part slightly, enough to convince me he is a numbers guy and my number matters. "Good. I like that."

Cassidy's eyes lift, the first sign of approval I've seen. Subtle, but unmistakable.

"I went to SMU," she said, almost as an aside. "Been watching your daughter, Claire, since her Vaughn Hill days. Six-two with guard skills. Strong first step, quick off the bounce, and that step-back three? That's what caught my attention. Not many players her size can create space like that." She said it flatly, like everything else, but I caught it. She already knew more than my bio.

McAllister's eyes narrow slightly. "What's your wheelhouse, Ben? What do clients call you for?"

"Complex commercial disputes. Mostly Fortune 500 companies and private equity firms. Contract fights, business divorces, shareholder claims. Cases that don't settle and don't go away. Last year alone, that brought in two and a half million."

He nods, as though the number meets expectations but does not surprise him. "And clients stick with you?"

"They have so far."

Cassidy crosses one leg over the other and studies me before speaking.

"I've read your bio. And a few of the articles. They paint a clear picture. You've built a reputation trying high-stakes commercial cases in state and federal courts. "I've read that you don't just try the cases. You shape them before you even get to trial, and you make them look simple when they're anything but."

I don't respond. I've heard it all before, but I want to see where she's going.

“They say you outwork everyone. That you don’t bluff, don’t chase headlines. That judges trust you because you come prepared, and juries trust you because you don’t pretend.”

She pauses, then adds, “With a practice like that, I’m surprised to see you’ve stayed in Dallas.”

I smile. “I’m a Cowboys fan, but that’s not the reason.”

She raises an eyebrow.

“I’m here because of the airport,” I say. “From DFW, I can get to San Diego, Seattle, Miami, or Boston in three to four hours. I don’t need to live in New York or LA to practice everywhere.”

McAllister jumps back in. “Cassidy says we should not waste your time. You already know we are the premier firm in the Southwest."

"I'm also aware of my ability to start where others finish."

He smiles faintly. “And you don’t consider yourself a Texas lawyer?”

“I consider myself a lawyer in Texas. That’s not always the same thing.”

Cassidy looks pleased, yet guarded. “We’re not just in Texas,” she says. “Not anymore. We have offices in Washington, New York, and Chicago, and we’re still adding lawyers.”

She gestures at the wall-sized screen, which hums to life. It's not the usual PowerPoint parade. There are maps showing office expansions in Los Angeles, charts of rising revenue, and business models with numbers that put mine to shame. McAllister pauses, giving the charts time to speak for themselves.

The numbers say plenty.

Hamilton Reed wants more, and fast. I could be the meanest, nastiest, and biggest asshole in all of Dallas, and they wouldn't care. I'm attractive to them, not because I'm a good guy or easy to work with, but because I have a big book of business, a national litigation practice, and I can add to their bottom line.

When I started, the law was a noble profession. Now it's a business. I have the clients with the money, and they want it. "California, I see."

Cassidy shakes her head, as if surprised I'm only now realizing they're doing business on the West Coast. Clients are national and even international now," she says. "We have to expand and add offices where they are."

McAllister leans forward with a look that shows he sees I can make a difference to the firm's bottom line. "Ben, you've got an impeccable track record. You come highly recommended. You're sharp and adaptable. We need those qualities if we're going to double our footprint in California. And Texas." He pauses long enough for me to understand what comes next. "We need partners who can double their business. Fast."

This isn't my first conversation with someone who wants more than they're saying. It's the first time the promise is backed by statistics and the number of zeros on the offer. I don't let the pause extend. "I understand," I say.

McAllister's grin says I do. "We're after the same thing here."

Cassidy closes her folder and pauses for a moment. "You'll have a contract in hand tomorrow morning."

On my way out, I pass a man in a cowboy hat heading in. He's got twice my belt buckle and enough swagger to suggest he doesn't need an appointment. I'm moving quickly, like I walked out with more than I expected, and no one's stopped me yet.

When I hit the street, I find my pace and keep moving. For a second, I think about turning around, going back up, and asking Cassidy if it's already too late to back out. But I don't. I already know the answer. I know what it will take to double my business, but, with a daughter who is a college basketball star at SMU, I'm not sure if I want to live that way.

By the time I get home, the question isn't whether I will take the offer. It is how I will explain it to Erin. She knows before I even say a word. I ease the front door shut, but Erin still hears me.

She's in the family room, the five o'clock news playing low. She doesn't turn when I come in. I know that move. Erin can always give me the floor by pretending I already have it.

She turns down the volume on the television. "You're home early," she says without looking over.

"It's only six," I say, hanging my keys in their usual place. My voice sounds too casual, even to me.

She waits a moment and then looks at me.

"You went," she says.

She doesn't mean the office. She means the interview.

I nod.

"And?"

"It went well."

"Well?"

"Offer's coming tomorrow morning." I pull out a chair and sit. The leather armrests are cool under my palms, familiar enough to steady me.

Erin watches me, weighing what I'm not saying. After nearly twenty-five years, she can tell when I'm selling. Right now, she hears my pitch.

I press ahead. "The firm has a big platform and a national presence, and they're adding more lawyers and offices. It'll help me keep and add the kind of clients I can't keep or get without offices everywhere. And it turns out that Cassidy, one of the lawyers who interviewed me, is one of Claire's fans. She's been following Claire since high school."

Erin raises an eyebrow. "So now we're making career decisions based on who watches Claire playing basketball?"

"No. But it didn't hurt. She already knew more about me than what was in my bio."

She nods slowly, not in agreement. It's more like she's following the script.

"And you said yes."

"I haven't signed a contract. But yeah."

She crosses her arms, eyes narrowing. "So you're ready to give up what you always said you liked best about your work? How many times have you said you'd never join a big firm because you'd lose control of your destiny?"

"That was before Mike screwed me."

"But does that mean you should run straight to the biggest firm in Dallas?"

"I don't see it that way."

"Of course you don't," she says softly. "Not yet."

Her words ring more true than I expect. I shift in my chair.

"Erin, this is the next step. I'm not staying with Mike after what happened. I can't keep turning down opportunities. The practice of law is rapidly changing. Boutiques are being eaten alive by the big firms. Fortune 500 clients expect their lawyer to have a deep bench and coverage all over the country. I either move with the change or lose major clients and get left behind."

"Left behind." She tests the phrase, almost to herself. "So this is about your clients and about not falling behind."

"No. It's about doing more for my best clients with the right resources."

She walks slowly around the island, fingertips brushing the counter. When she stops beside me, she stays standing, making me look up.

"You've spent your entire career building your name. Your clients hire you, not the firm you are with. You've chosen which clients to represent and which cases to handle. You've never needed a deep bench or offices all over the country."

"Until now."

"Until now? You didn't need it last month or the month before that."

Her voice isn't sharp, but it is steady. Erin has never needed volume to win an argument. Instead, she waits out the rationalizations.

"You know what I worry about?" she asks.

I look at her, waiting for her to tell me.

"I worry about what happens when the things you said your entire career that were important, stop mattering."

I don't answer. I want to finish our discussion.

"It's when everything becomes about the money. And you don't even realize what it's doing to you."

I exhale slowly, leaning back. "You think I'm going to change because I've joined a national law firm?"

She didn't blink. "I think you'll lose control of your practice, and you don't see how easy that will be."

Two weeks later, I set foot in my new office. Tessa Grant walks in behind me that first day, like she's done for the past twenty-five years. Hair pinned up, cardigan over her arm, eyes already scanning for trouble. She doesn't ask where her office is. She doesn't need to. By the time I finish shaking hands with someone I'll forget by lunch, she's already unpacked, rebooted the computer, and corrected the spelling on the nameplate outside my door.

Like Erin, Tessa doesn't want me to take this job. I'm pretty sure they compared notes. She told me over coffee in our old breakroom that joining Hamilton Reed feels like stepping onto a moving train that isn't slowing down. I get it. Like me, Tessa's going to lose some of her independence. But once I signed the offer, she packed up with me and never brought it up again. Tessa may not have a law degree, but she knows this world better than most partners. She knows me better than I know myself.

Everything in this office is expensive and designed to signal success. Not like my former Dallas office, where the walls were wood, the doors were solid, and the windows gave you a view of the city, not each other. Here, half the offices don't even have doors, and I'm convinced there's a secret scorecard where Cassidy tracks how long it takes me to find the light switch.

I see her every morning. She walks by my office without looking in. It takes me less than a week to realize that's a compliment. If I weren't holding up my end, she'd be staring.

Two weeks in, Brooke Chandler, a young Dallas partner in corporate, appears in my doorway. She doesn't knock or make small talk. She sets a thumb drive on my desk like it's a favor, but we both know it isn't. The file lists corporate clients who use other firms for litigation. If I bring them here, she gets credit. She's polite, strategic, and already playing the game everyone here understands.

Cassidy sees it. McAllister does too. They are not testing me. They are accelerating me. The partners know I am hungry. They know I have the capacity. What they are watching for is stamina.

I have already learned the rules. I know the difference between a pulse and anxiety. I can tell when caffeine stops being a boost and starts being a crutch. I have not learned when to call it a night. Maybe that is the point.

I tell myself it means I am getting stronger. I hope it does not mean I am going numb.

My inbox pings. The subject line is short: All Partners. Mandatory. 7:00 PM. There is no agenda. No explanation. Just that kind of punctuation that carries its own weight.

I close my laptop. I sit there for a moment longer. The floor is empty now. There is nothing left but ambition. I thought I was different. But the email reminds me of what I already suspect.

I am already one of them.

Chapter 2
The California Pitch

In football, small decisions shift momentum. In law, they decide who gets left behind.

#

After a long day, I leave my office and head toward the large conference room for the firm meeting. The sun is low on the horizon, casting long shadows through our office's glass windows. Most of the lawyers and staff on the floor have gone home.

I assume McAllister scheduled the firm-wide partner meeting for 7:00 PM Dallas time because the Los Angeles lawyers asked for it. That gives them time for their own staff to clear out before the meeting begins.

I find a seat at the table where Cassidy Knox, the partner who interviewed me, Preston Locke, senior statesman, and Brooke Chandler, the young, ambitious lawyer, are seated. Cassidy and Brooke greet me, and we talk briefly about the Dallas Stars playoff game. Locke sits still, hands folded, expression neutral.

McAllister stands and faces the room. He wastes no time.

"The Los Angeles law firm, Marwood Shaw, has agreed to join us. Having a Los Angeles office with top-notch lawyers will secure our place as a national player. I've already been contacted by legal publications that plan to write that we are the fastest-growing law firm in America."

Brooke is all ears when she hears that.

McAllister offers no further preamble. He provides no further justification. He delivers only the headline, which I interpret to mean he has the votes and it's a done deal.

McAllister clicks through a PowerPoint presentation prepared for the meeting. The screen fills with modern buildings, polished logos, and lists of high-profile clients. I glance at Locke. He says nothing. His face stays unreadable.

McAllister's voice is calm and assured.

"The LA lawyers have high-end clients who pay them top dollar. They bring big-paying clients and strong billing rates. Adding them makes us more profitable. It puts more money in each of your pockets."

The next slide appears. It is the logo of the Los Angeles firm, sleek, minimalist, and sharp. It does not invite trust. It commands attention. This is a firm that does not earn respect. It expects it.

I shift in my chair. The pitch is familiar. Ever since legal publications began ranking firms by profits per partner, headcount, and office locations, firms have chased money and size.

Erin had warned me that I was joining a firm where I would not decide what happens. Other than casting a vote, I am a passenger.

He continues without pause.

"Los Angeles gives us everything we lack. They are dominant players in tech, media, and entertainment law. This is how we expand practices, grow nationally, and climb the rankings."

The next slide brings up a live video feed.

Bianca Rivers sits beside Evan Marston, perfectly framed in the California video feed. The lighting flatters her, but she does not depend on it. She sits with a composed posture, her voice calm and clear. Every word is delivered with the confidence of someone who expects to be remembered.

Evan speaks first.

"This is an incredible opportunity for both firms. Together, we are stronger and better positioned for what is coming."

I catch his phrasing. Not if. When. In his mind, this is inevitable, exactly what I expected.

"I'll let Bianca share her ideas with you."

Without a beat's hesitation, Bianca’s voice flows. "This is exciting," she pronounces, a polished warmth in her tone. "Together, we can add value for clients, attract new ones, and increase profitability. You bring reputation and depth. We bring scale and innovation."

It's a performance, undoubtedly, yet executed with such fluid grace, it's impossible to pinpoint where the script ends and instinct begins. She knows precisely how to set the hook: a touch of deference, then the irresistible pull of advantage. Her smile lingers, her words gliding on.

She takes a moment to let us digest what she is saying. I look around, and several Dallas partners are all attention and waiting for more.

“Some of our best deals have started over martinis at Tower Bar,” she says. “Ask Trent Blackwood." There's a faint, almost private resonance in her voice, hinting at a past steeped in power and risks no one talked about.

Everyone knows that Trent Blackwood is a tech billionaire known for his brilliance and famous for throwing parties in Malibu that start with champagne and end with silence. People talk about the guest lists, but not about what goes on behind the gates. He chooses which ventures to fund and which companies to crush, and moves through Los Angeles like a man who knows nothing can touch him.

Rumors follow him. There are whispers of NDAs, sealed court records, and threats that never make the news. No one has ever pinned anything on him. She laughs at something Evan says. For a moment, her eyes shift, and the smile doesn't quite reach them. It's gone as quickly. I can't tell what it was, but it didn't match the laugh.

Bianca Rivers brought him in. That may have been her ticket to making partner. Or maybe it was the way she played a hand no one else saw coming.

When I first heard whispers about the LA deal, I looked her up. Los Angeles Business had run a profile on her, with photos alongside Trent Blackwood. I read about her East LA background, her rise to partner in record time, and her spot on the Top 40 Lawyers Under 40 list. The article called her ambitious, fearless, and strategic. Watching her now, I believe every word.

Whatever her colleagues in Los Angeles thought of her before, they started treating her differently after that. Maybe it was the client. Perhaps it was how she got him. Or maybe it was something she knew, something no one ever proved.

Partners around the table shift. Some lean in. Others glance at one another. I do neither.

Bianca doesn't raise her voice. But when I look around, I see my partners watching her. Whatever it is, she knows how to hold a room. Her tone never changes, steady as a closing argument. At one point, her expression shifts, like she's looking at someone in Dallas. Maybe McAllister. The look lasts long enough to make me think she's one reason he's pushing the merger.

The older partners stare at her. The younger ones try not to. Bianca knows what they see, and she uses it. She's not reacting. She knows all eyes are on her. I've seen lawyers like her before. But not often. And not many who could hold a room full of skeptical Dallas lawyers without raising their voice. Her presence alone holds their attention.

After a few minutes of Bianca warming up the crowd, Evan speaks.

Dominate and make more money. That is the message.

They know what to say and how to say it. But their ease unnerves me. Bianca jokes about closing deals over martinis. It gets a laugh, but not from me. That's not how we've done business in Texas.

I scan the room. The younger partners are smiling. The older ones sit still. Cassidy stays rigid, her eyes on the screen.

Bianca's final words ring out.

"We look forward to meeting everyone in person soon. This is the beginning of something big."

*

Bianca's Turn: Taking the Room

Los Angeles – On camera, same moment

Let them think it's a pitch. I'm here to persuade.

They want our big-name entertainment and tech clients' hefty fees and multimillion-dollar profits per partner. The kind of specialized, high-margin practice that turns heads and inflates balance sheets. Some in Texas haven't admitted it yet.

Evan plays the room with his customary smooth delivery. I've seen him use it on potential new clients. He thinks Dallas wants a handshake and a smile. I suspect he's right. I can see it on their faces on the screen. McAllister is hot to add us. They need us more than we need them. If we don't join Hamilton Reed, at least twenty other firms would line up to offer us more.

They want confidence, but more than that, they want explosive growth. The kind that doesn't come from playing safe.

As Evan and I planned, it's my turn to shift the energy.

I start talking. A few in the Dallas office perk up when they see me. I can't see the lawyers in the other offices clearly, but I know how this plays. This is an audition, and I know the part. I've played versions of this role before. Once, in front of a billionaire's private legal team. Once, in a glass-walled room where I was the only woman and the only one still standing at the end.

I give them a name they'll recognize. Trent Blackwood, the billionaire tech company founder. He's a visionary, and the kind of man who keeps lawyers like me close, especially when the stories get dangerous. He dominates in boardrooms, courtrooms, and the headlines, and generates major fees from his frequent legal disputes.

The ones who know, lean in. The ones who don't will ask later. That's all I need.

I once watched a general counsel lose his job three weeks after underestimating me. He never saw the press release coming. Most don't.

I don't need them to like me. I need them to remember me.

As far as I'm concerned, we're not merging to build something better. We're merging to take control. And the ones still watching that screen?

They'll either adapt to what's coming. Or they'll become the reason we rewrite the rules.

*

The screen fades to black. I'm back in the Dallas conference room, seated at the long table with Locke, Cassidy, Brooke, and other partners I don't know. No one moves. Someone shifts in their chair. Cassidy sets down her pen but says nothing. My colleagues and I are trying to digest what we heard.

McAllister finally speaks.

"Thoughts?"

He's not really seeking input. He's made up his mind, and he has the votes to make the merger happen. He's checking boxes to claim he sought feedback.

Brooke speaks first.

"This is a perfect fit. Our corporate clients have offices in California. We need to be where they are doing business."

The younger partners jump in quickly with their support. The pace of their agreement feels rehearsed. One mentions that LA will give us an edge in attracting talent. It sounds less like a calculated strategy and more like a reaction to the idea of having an office in Los Angeles, thinking it makes us relevant.

Tom's voice breaks through, low and steady.

"We built this firm on personal connections and trust. That's our foundation and our firm culture. This merger will change who we are."

A few heads nod. Locke among them.

Cassidy speaks next.

"Growth without preserving our values is not growth. It is abandonment."

McAllister does not respond. He doesn't need to. His silence is the answer, and his side is already moving.

I stay quiet, watching the room take sides. When the eyes turn to me, I give them nothing. It’s too early to choose sides. A clear line forms: the young lawyers, seeing only opportunity in this leap of faith, and the old lawyers, seeing only a threat to everything they've built in their firm.

The meeting ends without a vote. But everyone knows where it is going.

Two partners lean in toward McAllister. Others stand in clusters, voices low but urgent. Younger partners gather around McAllister and Brooke. Cassidy and Tom Whitfield whisper near the door. It’s clear they don’t want to add the LA bunch, but they know McAllister has the votes.

As I step into the hallway, a few younger partners approach me.

"Exciting, right?"

"Big opportunity."

"It's a big move," I say. "A lot to consider."

They nod politely and move on. They were not asking for my opinion. They were checking my alignment.

The next morning, I reopen the merger documents. Charts and projections blur together. Everything points in one direction. The message is to keep moving forward. Whether you want it or not.

Opposing McAllister would mean isolation. Supporting him feels like surrender.

Erin's words come back to me.

"This is how it starts. You don't choose it. You get used to it."

I reread my draft email. My cursor hovers.

"After reviewing the materials, I support moving forward."

I don't necessarily think that is the right choice. But, going along with it keeps me from being cut out of the room.

I click send.

By noon, the announcement goes out.

"Merger exploration approved."

McAllister follows up.

"Ben, I want to let you know that I appreciate your support."

I close the message and turn toward the window. The Dallas skyline looks vast and indifferent.

Appreciate your support. The phrase lingers. I am aligned with those who want to grow now. In today's legal market, every law firm wants to grow bigger, to impress clients, attract talented lawyers, and open offices in all the major cities in the country. I try cases all across the country, so having offices in other states appeals to me.

But Erin's warning returns.

"You may not even notice when you start becoming someone else."

I turn away from the window and face the screen again. The merger is no longer a proposal.

It's a done deal.

And, despite Erin's worries, part of me is excited to have the opportunity to try cases in California. That may be the most dangerous part.

Chapter 3
When Lines Blur

In sports and law, the rules don't really change. But the referees get softer, the players get bolder, and soon, everyone's playing a different game.

#

Even before the elevator doors open all the way, I hear voices that are sharper than usual for this early hour. There's a buzz on the floor.

The doors slide open. A group of Los Angeles lawyers stands ahead, already settled in.

Their laughter carries down the hall. They stand in small groups, talking loudly, jackets off, ties loosened. It is not how Dallas lawyers usually arrive in the morning.

The California lawyers have arrived. They don't look like the lawyers I see in Dallas.

I step off the elevator and the split is obvious. The older partners watch from a distance, arms crossed. Preston Locke stands nearby, close enough to hear them but not quite in the huddle. A low murmur passes between them, and I catch the phrase "McAllister's chasing rankings again," a sentiment I've heard whispered for weeks.

Brooke Chandler is already deep in conversation with two of the LA lawyers, name-dropping judges and clients. A few other young partners join her, their energy less about welcome and more about auditioning for a role in whatever power structure comes next.

I overhear snippets of their conversation. They talk about suites at Dodger Stadium and Lakers games, golf at Riviera, and impossible-to-get reservations in Venice or Brentwood.

"Almost missed our flight," Evan jokes. Bianca flashes a grin. "Hope Dallas brought its A-game."

The older partners aren't happy, and I can tell they're wary of their established culture being steamrolled. The younger ones, perhaps envisioning a faster track to wealth and prestige by adding the lucrative LA office, offer a more eager, welcome.

Brooke spots me and waves. She has a smile on her face. "Ben! You must be buzzing with excitement about what the LA office can do for your practice."

"Big changes," I reply, trying to sound neutral. "It should certainly be interesting." I'm not sure how it will be interesting, only that the Dallas culture at the firm could not be more different than the anything-goes culture of the LA office.

By midmorning, Evan and Bianca have taken over the main conference room. Their presentation, all sleek slides and confident pronouncements, sounds less like a discussion and more like a declaration.

"This isn't a merger," Evan says, leaning back like he is in control. "This is becoming a major player."

Bianca moves with a restless energy. Her words are sharp and decisive. "Los Angeles brings the tech and entertainment clients. Texas brings energy clients. Together, we can be in the AmLaw Top 100 law firms."

The old guard remains silent. Cassidy Knox leans back, arms crossed, her gaze fixed on the presenters, a clear look of disdain in her eyes.

Bianca presses her point, her tone challenging. "Clients want agility. They don't care about tradition. They care about results."

I glance at Cassidy. She doesn't flinch, but her arms fold tighter. She knows that really means do whatever it takes to get results and move on. A ripple of laughter breaks the tension. Some of The younger partners nod, perhaps trying to demonstrate they're in sync. The veterans stay impassive, their silence serving as another weighty counterpoint.

Preston Locke looks over at me as Bianca speaks, a fleeting expression that suggests he believes results shouldn't come at the expense of established ethical boundaries.

I keep my expression neutral, but my mind is racing. Even though our law firm is acquiring the LA firm, they act more like they are taking over.

McAllister's hunger for the rankings is driving this, and I'm not sure the Texas way of practicing law will survive.

I see Brooke and other younger partners smiling, and I hear low grumbles from the white- and gray-haired lawyers. They are against adding the LA office. It's been evident from the beginning. I get it. The culture they have known hasn't vanished overnight. What they dislike the most is that what they built isn't even mentioned in the conversation anymore.

That evening, the heavy door closes behind the waiter, cutting off the restaurant's hum. Inside, the room is filled with low voices and clinking wine glasses. I step into the room and watch. Brooke Chandler stands near the entrance with a drink, watching who walks in and who doesn't.

Evan Marston and Bianca Rivers stand in the corner, speaking quietly while others gather around them. Earlier today, they wore tailored suits designed to impress. Tonight, they've traded them for

California casual, still expensive and intended to leave an impression. The older Dallas partners have not shown up, but several young ones have.

Brooke spots me and waves. “Ben! Glad you made it.” Her eyes land on me. She is already gauging my reaction. I nod and scan the guest list. The younger guard is here. The ambitious associates are too. I am alone. No spouses. Erin was not invited, and I doubt that was an oversight.

“Nice setup, Brooke,” I say. She is running point. The pitch continues without pause.

“It’s the start,” she replies.

Evan and Bianca join us, their half-empty wine glasses suggesting they’ve already made themselves comfortable. Evan nods like a man who assumes the room was waiting for him. “Didn’t expect Texas to play this close to the vest, Ben.” A hint of playful challenge in his voice.

Bianca laughs, not because she thinks that’s funny. She’s watching to see who’s with her. “First time for everything.” She raises her glass, her gaze briefly locking with mine. “To new alliances.”

More Texas lawyers arrive, a mix of eager juniors and cautious seniors, wanting to hear more. The missing partners are their way of protesting the firm's fracturing. McAllister planned to be absent so his lieutenants could set the tone. I sense that many in the room have unfinished agendas.

Brooke moves through the room, a seasoned diplomat, her voice effortlessly guiding conversations. Evan and Bianca hold court at the far end, as if they're already running the firm. Evan gestures. "Ben, come join us."

I watch who huddles with Evan, who hangs back, and who keeps checking Bianca's face before they laugh. I'm seated next to the younger partners who are hungry to make more money and have less to lose if the merger goes south.

The conversation shifts. Stories get looser. The laughter gets louder. Lines blur, and no one seems bothered. This isn't how we've done things at Hamilton Reed.

Bianca leans in, lowering her voice like she is letting me in on a secret. A tale of a tech billionaire's legal disaster was barely avoided. "Money solves these kinds of problems, Ben."

Laughter ripples around the table. A few of the younger Texans look impressed, and eager to fit in.

I don't object. No one objects. That's the part that stays with me.

Bianca lifts her glass. "We can do it all," she says. "Once Texas catches up."

Evan grins. "Or maybe Texas won't. Ready for that?"

I don't answer. Laughter fills the space where a response should be.

The wine keeps coming. Stories get looser. Voices rise. People shift their chairs closer to Evan and Bianca.

They don't look like guests anymore.

Evan tells a story about a venture-backed startup that tried to sue Blackwood for breach of fiduciary duty. "We made a motion to dismiss based on our arbitration clause. It was granted, and we won in arbitration."

Their world comes across as both alluring and unsettling.

More stories, more laughter at the expense of unseen others. I laugh along, even as something about their acceptance puts me on edge.

By the time Brooke's parting words, "This is the start," send us into the night, my head swims with conflicting impressions. Adaptation or selling out? Their rules are different. Am I even playing the same game?

Walking to my car, I remind myself that McAllister's absence and my invitation were all parts of a calculated strategy. Am I meant to be their leveraging point? Their conduit for dissenters? The thought is chilling. How much of myself am I willing to bend? And what will it cost?

After a restless night, the next morning I step out of the elevator and head down the hall. Cassidy is waiting outside my office, arms crossed. She does not move when she sees me. The unease from last night's forced laughter and too-casual conversations stays with me. Her eyes, sharp and direct, settle on mine, demanding more than a polite greeting.

"Busy morning, Ben?" Her dry tone slices through the stillness.

I try to be nonchalant. "Looks like you've got me cornered, Cassidy." My heart rate ticks up a notch.

"Got a minute?" It's not a request. She remains still.

"Quite a dinner last night," she says, a thin layer of sarcasm coating the words.

I avoid her gaze, focusing on the carpet. She knows the guest list.

"Predictably California."

She doesn't respond right away, waiting. I have nothing valuable to say.

“They’re moving fast.” A sharp edge enters her voice.

“Enthusiastic.” The word is flimsy even to me.

Her eyes narrow, assessing. “And Texas?”

I shrug, a pathetic attempt at indifference. “Some are too eager.”

“Seems they’ve decided who matters.” Her gaze doesn't waver.

I don’t reply. The exclusion stings more than I want to admit.

“Thought they’d drag out the charade.” Her arms remain a shield. “Insider jokes become insider deals, Ben. Fast.”

“Maybe you will have more time.” The reassurance sounds hollow.

“You don’t believe that.” Her bluntness hits harder than I expect.

She glances down the empty hallway. She almost smiles, but it doesn’t last. “This is how it starts. Today, wine-fueled bravado. Tomorrow, it's lawsuit threats and investor panic. They play it loose. Gray areas turn dark fast.” The forced laughter from last night echoes in my memory.

"Ben, I know they've pulled you in." She leans closer, her voice low and urgent. "What you thought was dinner was a line in the sand, and you crossed it. Are you ready for that?"

I don't respond.

"Or are you along for the ride?" Her gaze is unwavering, dissecting my uncertainty.

I look away, then back. I can see the disappointment in her eyes. "Cassidy, I see what you're saying." My voice is even, but I lack conviction.

She shakes her head slowly. "You know what's coming, Ben. This won't stop at dinners."

"It's a done deal," I say.

"What do you think we can do now?"

I don't answer.

She waits.

Then she unfolds her arms. "How long before it's too late for you?"

"Maybe never."

"Maybe soon."

She turns and walks away. Her footsteps fade down the hall.

The lock clicks behind me. The building is silent except for the hum of the lights. I should be home. Erin would have called this before it happened.

The merger notes on my screen offer no comfort. We're a bigger firm now, making headlines in every legal rag, but nothing feels right. Erin's call from earlier echoes in my mind. She'd asked about dinner, sensed my unease without me saying a word. She won't say "I told you so," but I know she's thinking it.

And the next part? That's the hardest to admit. What if she's right?

I lean back, the chair groaning about where things are headed. I try to shake it off, but it clings. Everything's moving too fast, and everyone seems to be rushing along with it. I remember that dinner, letting their attention flatter me, and now I'm disgusted with myself.

"*What if it isn't?*" Erin's voice, again. I shove the papers aside. The shift has begun. No turning back now. I'm already thinking about the meetings tomorrow.

Better get used to it, a cynical voice tells me. I straighten the papers on my desk, a useless gesture against the internal chaos. Outside, the city glitters, the firm's faint logo on the skyline a cold reminder of the world I'm in. How long can I stand between two worlds before I'm simply gone?

Chapter 4

The New Order

In sports, sometimes the field shifts beneath your feet, and you're still playing the same game, but the rules feel different. Likewise, in law, the job doesn't change, but the pressure does, and so do the people who rise to the top.

#

It's Monday morning. I leave home early, coffee in hand, hit the gym, shower, dress, and get to the office by seven.

I work on a case in the quiet of my office. It's the kind of silence that helps me get work done before the noise starts. By nine, laughter and small talk drift down the hall. I step out. The laughter feels out of place this early.

I walk toward the noise. Evan Marston and Bianca Rivers are already in the break room, laughing like they've been here forever. Evan hands a coffee to a junior associate with an exaggerated flourish, like he's pouring champagne at a private party.

Brooke Chandler, the young Dallas partner, is right there with them, laughing loudest, her hand brushing Evan's arm as she throws her head back at something he says. Other younger partners hover nearby, no longer even pretending to miss the old Texas formality.

I stop inside the doorway, cup in hand, and watch. The older partners stiffen as they pass, nodding but never stopping.

Bianca introduces me to Rachel Wolfe, one of the LA associates. We trade a few quick words about a matter she's staffing. Rachel blends in fast.

The break room isn't built for this many people, especially not this kind of crowd. Too many bodies packed close, too much noise for this early. Someone brought pastries, but no one touches them. Nobody's here to eat. They're here to be seen.

I linger at the edges, invisible but present. I watch Brooke shift closer to Evan, her voice pitched high enough to stand out. Even partners who used to cling tight to tradition seem tempted now. Their eyes flick toward the group, weighing whether to join or disappear entirely.

I watch the younger partners lean in, hungry for every word. The older ones keep their distance. If you're not laughing along, you're already on the outside.

The chairs are pulled into a loose circle. No structure, no seating hierarch.

Brooke finally notices me. Her grin stretches wide. “Ben, is that California coffee?”

I raise my cup slightly. “Still Texas coffee. For now.”

A few people laugh.

Brooke waves me closer. “Come on. You need to loosen up.”

The group opens just enough for me to step in. I sit on the edge of a chair.

Bianca turns toward me. “We've been wondering where you were.”

Evan nods. “You're on LA time now, right?”

Their tone is light. The message isn't. Adopt the pace or fall behind.

“I try to keep up,” I say.

The conversation moves quickly after that. Celebrity clients. Emergency settlements. Judges who understand discretion.

The younger partners hang on every word. The older ones drift away.

Bianca’s phone buzzes. She glances at the screen and stands.

“Give me a minute.”

She and Evan walk toward one of the glass offices along the hall. Evan pauses in the doorway and looks back at me.

"Ben."

He gestures for me to follow.

Inside the office Bianca is already on the call.

Her voice carries easily through the room.

"Relax," she tells the client. "We'll keep it out of the headlines."

I stop just inside the doorway.

Evan leans against the desk, listening.

Bianca speaks with complete confidence. Judges. Filing strategies. Timing. It sounds rehearsed, like she has run this play a hundred times.

Evan glances at me.

"Ben," he says quietly.

"How creative can you be?"

The question hangs in the room. It is not about skill. It is about whether I am willing to cross the line they are inviting me to cross.

Bianca's pitch keeps rolling. She tells the client everything will be discreet and smooth. It sounds rehearsed, like something she has done countless times. She names the judges without hesitation, as if each one is part of a plan already in motion. Nothing in her delivery wavers. Maybe for her, this is routine.

"We'll keep it out of the headlines," she says. Her confidence is impressive. She makes it sound routine. Like none of this is unusual.

I hesitate at the edge of the glass office. They are not whispering. Anyone walking by could hear every word. They do not care. That sends a clearer message than anything they say aloud.

Evan watches me, still settled in his chair but sharp as a blade. He lets Bianca do the selling, but he is closing the deal. I see it in the way he studies me, reading every flicker of my reaction.

I step closer, staying careful. I keep enough distance to avoid committing, but they have already pulled me in. Not with force. With expectation.

Bianca wraps up her call, tossing out big names and familiar judges. She speaks casually, with a confidence that makes me uneasy. This is not how we practiced law back home.

I glance toward the hallway. The sound carries. It always does in this building. They are not hiding, which makes it worse. This is not a secret. This is how they operate.

Evan's eyes stay locked on me. "You know the Texas courts," he says. His voice drops slightly, making the question personal. His words sound friendly, but they land like a challenge.

I get it. They are not asking if I am capable. They are asking if I am willing.

"We know our way around," I say carefully. I keep my tone steady and neutral. It is the only safe ground left. I will not commit. But I also will not say no.

Evan nods slowly, satisfied. His expression tells me everything. I passed. Or I failed. Maybe both.

"Exactly what we hoped," he says. He smiles, but there is nothing warm in it. He knows I am in now. At least halfway.

Bianca clicks off the call and straightens in her chair. "You're in good hands," she says, her voice light. The words linger in the air. The confidence in the room is heavy now, impossible to ignore.

I stand there longer than I should. They move on fast, swapping stories about past settlements and clever deals. The conversation shifts easily, but that moment doesn't fade. It clings. The edge of it stays sharp, cutting through their casual tone. I know what happened, even if they act like it's already forgotten.

I walk away, finally, the laughter still floating behind me. Evan and Bianca are already onto the next thing. I am still back there, replaying what they said and what I agreed to without saying much at all.

Back at my office, I sit down and stare at the skyline. I am used to being steady. To clear lines and predictable games.

How creative can you be?

I focus on that question now. They don't care about creativity. They care about compliance. The lines blur until they vanish.

I crossed one today. I know it. Even if no one says it out loud.

For them, this was routine. For me, it was something else. Something heavier.

I step away from my desk and close my eyes. I hear Bianca's voice, Evan's challenge, and my own reply. I am part of this now.

I know the difference. I still see it for now.

Chapter 5

The Test

In sports, once the rules loosen, the best players push even further. In law, it's no different. Once someone crosses the line and gets rewarded, everybody starts stepping over it.

#

The elevator doors part. Brooke is already there, leaning against the wall. She smiles when she sees me, but there's something sharp behind it.

"Drinks?" she asks, voice light and mischievous. She steps closer, lowering her voice. "For fun."

The way she says it leaves no doubt. This isn't a casual invitation. It's a test. An expectation wrapped in playful ease.

I hesitate. Erin flashes into my mind, her questions and quiet skepticism already forming in my head. Brooke senses the pause. She tilts her head, eyes narrowing.

"You're not going to bail, are you?" she teases, daring me to prove her wrong. The way she says it, I am either a coward or a colleague. To me, that's a choice I'd prefer not to make.

By the time I step into the hotel bar, I already regret my decision. I should have said no. Erin's face and Cassidy's warning should have been enough. But the way Brooke asked made the cost of staying home feel higher than I wanted to pay. I told myself it was only one drink.

Laughter ricochets across the dim room, riding waves of low music and pulsing energy. Conversations layer on top of one another, private and public at once. The room hums with unspoken possibilities.

Evan spots me first. He waves, his grin wide and warm, instantly dissolving any chance I had to slip away.

"Didn't think you'd make it," he calls, voice easy but edged. His hand lands firmly on my shoulder when I reach him, sealing the moment. This is more than a casual drink.

Bianca is at the bar, her dress cut low enough to captivate every man who passes by. She holds a drink lazily, turning slightly as our eyes meet. Her expression shifts to a half-smile and half-challenge.

There's a sharpness beneath that smile, the kind of calm confidence that quietly dares to see how far I'll go. I'm aware she's sizing me up, and yeah, part of me wants to go for it. But more than that, I don't want to give in to the temptation.

"Thought you'd bail," she says, her voice like silk over steel. Her words pull me forward before I can process them. She doesn't move much, but her shoulder shifts slightly in my direction. It's a minor adjustment, enough to catch my attention. I'd bet she's practiced that move with men more than once.

I slide into the group, greeted as though I belong. Their acceptance is fast and warm. Too warm.

They know how to make it look easy. They know precisely what they are doing.

Around us, younger partners and associates blend into the crowd. Brooke stands front and center, laughing freely, touching Evan's arm as if it's the most natural thing in the world. She leans in when she speaks, closes whatever space is left, makes herself unavoidable. Around her, people adjust, shifting to accommodate her presence.

Bianca doesn't do that.

She's at the bar, still, one shoulder angled just enough to command the room without claiming it. She doesn't reach for anyone. She doesn't have to. Men look, hesitate, and look again, unsure whether they're invited. When her eyes meet mine, she doesn't smile right away. She lets the moment sit until I'm the one exposed.

I drift closer without meaning to. Her shoulder brushes mine. Light. Intentional. The kind of touch that makes you notice.

She speaks softly, her voice barely cutting through the music.

“Do you know what makes a secret powerful, Ben?” she asks.

She lets the question hang for a moment, then continues. "It’s how quietly it changes everything."

She keeps her eyes on mine, allowing the words to settle. She is not pushing. She is giving me room to step closer.

She leans in until her perfume hits. It is sweet and heavy, and clearly chosen on purpose.

She didn’t leave anything to chance. Her hair is perfect. Her dress is tight and short enough to make a point. Her heels aren’t worn for comfort. They give her height, stillness, and the advantage of being looked at while deciding whether to look back.

I don’t step back. Pulling away would look weak. And right now, I don’t want to.

Her words slide in easily. I tell myself this is harmless. It’s drinks and talk, and nothing more.

But I stay. The drinks keep coming. Laughter gets louder. I stop pretending I’m not part of it.

Her hand finds mine again. Casual this time. It lingers. I let it.

Each touch pulls me in. I keep telling myself I can leave whenever I want. I'm wrong.

I catch her watching me when she thinks I won't notice. Not playful now. Calculating. She knows I like the attention. Too much.

She doesn't want me. Not really. She wants to know if she can make me want her. That's the point. Men like me are easier to read once they think they're being chosen.

And for a while, I play it.

I check the time. Tipoff was twenty minutes ago. SMU vs. Virginia Tech. Claire texted this morning: Big game tonight, Dad. You coming?

I said I'd try.

Bianca leans in again, her voice low and smooth. "You don't have to be the good guy forever. Not tonight."

She steps closer, watching to see if I move away. I don't. She reaches for my elbow and smiles. Bianca has my attention.

I still don't move. I haven't had a woman try to seduce me in a long time. I'd be lying if I said it didn't flatter me.

Then I step back.

"My daughter's playing tonight. SMU. She's one of their starters."

Bianca's smile falters, slightly. She wasn't expecting that.

"You're leaving for a basketball game?"

"That's right."

Her face resets. Cool again. But something behind her eyes sharpens.

"Suit yourself," she says.

I walk away. Not fast, not slow. But, enough to make sure I don't turn back.

Outside, the night air hits hard. The door closes behind me, but her grip is still there. Not physical. Something sharper.

Bianca had already decided what to do with me.

And for too long tonight, I let her win.

I've already missed half of Claire's game. I can only hope she hasn't looked up and seen my empty seat.

I get in the car and turn on the radio. SMU's up by five. I drive faster than I should.

Traffic near campus is heavier than I'd like. I pull into my reserved space behind Moody, park, and make my way to the arena as the teams are heading back onto the court. I slip into the seat next to Erin. She doesn't say anything at first. Instead, she gives me one of her looks.

"I'm sorry," I say quietly. "I had to spend time with the new lawyers from Los Angeles. I got here as fast as I could."

She looks straight ahead. The second half is starting. My excuse doesn't land.

Claire is on the floor, directing traffic. She's wearing number 10, the number she's worn since grade school. At six-foot-three, she's taller than most point guards, but she moves like she's smaller. She's quick on her feet, steady with either hand, always seeing the floor. She passes to the wing and keeps moving. The forward hesitates, sees Claire pop open at the top of the arc, and gives it back to her. Claire doesn't hesitate. She knocks down a deep three as the shot clock expires. The crowd roars. She turns and runs back on defense like she's done it a thousand times.

I look around the section. A few rows up, I spot Cassidy. She's wearing a black blazer, arms crossed. Her face doesn't give anything away, but she sees me. Then she looks back toward the court.

I stay until the final buzzer. Claire leads all scorers with twenty-four points and adds seven assists. As she leaves the court, she looks up, finds us, and blows a kiss toward our row. Erin smiles and waves back. I do the same.

We walk out together. Erin doesn't say anything about me missing the first half. Not yet. Our cars are parked side by side. We each get in and drive home.

We pull into the driveway within seconds of each other. Neither of us speaks.

Inside, she sets her purse on the counter and turns to face me. Her arms cross, but she stays calm.

"I smelled it at the game," she says. "That perfume."

I stop inside the room.

"Tom Ford Soleil Blanc," she adds. "She was wearing it."

Her voice is even, without emotion. She doesn't need to explain.

I answer too quickly. "It was a crowded bar. Everyone was packed in."

She doesn't blink. "You missed half your daughter's basketball game while in a crowded bar? You should shower."

She walks past me and heads down the hall. She doesn't accuse me or raise her voice. Instead, she creates a space between us that says more than words ever could.

I stand there for a moment, caught between the night I should not have let happen and the home I promised to protect. Then I follow her. She didn't need to say more, and that is what makes it worse.

I don't sleep well. I wake before the alarm and drive in early, hoping the quiet will help me find my footing. It doesn't. The parking lot is still half empty when I pull in, but the lights are on upstairs. I ride the elevator alone, watching the numbers climb, the silence doing nothing to settle me.

Cassidy waits for me outside my office, arms folded tight, eyes fixed ahead. I don't see her until I'm almost past, and by then, it's too late.

"Claire played well," she says, her voice dry. "You walked in and only caught the second half."

I stop.

"Long night?" she adds. The way she says it leaves no doubt that she knows exactly where I was before the game.

I keep it casual. "You could say that."

She steps into my path, steady and deliberate. She gets right to the point without hesitation.

"You have a minute?" she asks, though we both know she's already taken it.

Her eyes narrow slightly. "I hear you were having fun."

She says it like an accusation dressed in sarcasm. I shrug, trying to play it down. "It was nothing."

Cassidy shakes her head slowly. "You believe that?"

Her stare is too direct. I look away, shifting my weight. She presses forward anyway.

"You think you're still in control?"

The question hangs there, cutting deeper than I want to admit. I force a smile. "I know what I'm doing."

Cassidy leans in, voice low and even. "They're working you, Ben. You don't even see it."

Her words echo louder than I expect. I swallow, glancing down the hall, as though escape might still be possible.

"It's under control," I say, voice flat and unconvincing.

She steps even closer. Her words land hard. "They didn't invite you to dinner. They asked for your commitment."

I shift again. Defensive. "It was one night."

"No, Ben." Her tone softens slightly, but it's sharper for it. "That's not how this works."

She doesn't raise her voice, but the pressure is there. I can hear it between her words.

Cassidy crosses her arms again. The conversation is almost over, but not yet finished. "You think you can walk away clean?"

"I do," I say quickly, too quickly.

She doesn't move. "Maybe it's too late."

Her certainty leaves no room for argument. She turns to go, but I call out anyway.

"You're wrong."

Cassidy pauses at the corner, one hand already on her hip, half turned back toward me. She offers the smallest of smiles, but there's no warmth in it.

"I'm not," she says quietly.

Then she's gone, her footsteps fading down the hallway.

I stand there a moment longer, watching the space she left behind. Her words stick, impossible to shake as I step back into my office and close the door behind me.

Hours blur in meetings and calls. By evening, the floor is quiet again. The click of the lock ends the workday. I can focus now.

My office is quiet. I sit at my desk, lit only by the glow of my monitor, replaying the past twenty-four hours. I think about Bianca's subtle invite, and Cassidy's words.

I should have said more before I left the bar. I keep thinking about it, wondering if it would have changed anything.

Now those moments stack up, like the papers on my desk. Uneven. Unfinished.

And I know where I should be. Erin is home, probably cleaning up after dinner or flipping through papers, still waiting for me to keep the promises I made months ago. "You'll still be you," I told her when I joined this place. I believed it then.

Now?

Erin's voice drifts in again, breaking the quiet. Are you sure this is still you?

She never accuses. She waits, watching while I think about how to respond. There's no comfort anywhere in it.

Cassidy's words echo: They didn't invite you. They made you part of their team.

I get her point, and I don't like it.

I let them pull me in and I liked it.

That's what scares me most.

Chapter 6
The Favor

In sports, a favor means passing the ball instead of taking the shot. In law, it's never that clean. A favor is a setup. You do what's asked, and sooner or later, someone comes to collect.

#

Bianca's assistant calls and tells me to meet her in the Wilshire office. It's a request, but really it's a direction. The kind Bianca expects you to follow without question.

I fly in the night before. I'm the only one from Dallas here.

Her corner office overlooks Westwood. The glass is tinted, but the heat still creeps in. I wait outside while she finishes a call with one of her clients. She waves me in, without smiling.

"I need you to handle something," she says before a greeting or small talk.

I look at the caption of the redwell on her desk: Savannah Robinson v. Trent Blackwood.

"Another harassment suit?"

Bianca does not answer right away. She studies me. "You are going to handle this one."

"There are thirty litigators in your office. Why me? I am a Texas lawyer, and the case is in Los Angeles."

She slides the file across the desk. "Because I trust you, and Trent trusts me."

That is the answer, but not the reason. Trust cuts both ways. I've learned that the hard way, and I don't give mine easily.

I flip through the complaint. The intent is obvious. This is a sexual harassment claim designed for maximum publicity, drafted as much for the media as for the court.

#

The plaintiff, Savannah Robinson, was already a familiar face from the news cycle. Twenty-eight, a striking blond, she graduated from Harvard Business School with honors and drew multiple high-profile offers from industry titans. Tech competitors claimed that Blackwood had personally poached her, promising a directorship of Strategic Partnerships to lead global expansion, a plum role that fit her ambition and sharp intellect.

Yet, according to the complaint, the nature of her employment changed in ways that were impossible to ignore. Blackwood allegedly isolated her, systematically blurring the lines between professional and personal. Career advancement, the filing asserted, became inexorably tied to granting him private access.

The narrative spiraled through accounts of private jet flights, luxurious five-star resorts, and late-night meetings that progressively morphed into something far more intimate and coercive. Graphic text messages were cited, along with chilling excerpts from emails exchanged after her attempts to sever the relationship.

The complaint culminated in a specific night in Napa, where, she alleged, they were entirely alone, and Blackwood's pressure turned explicitly physical. Dates, locations, and language that left nothing to the imagination were meticulously laid out, ensuring it resonated equally in the courtroom and on the evening news.

I look up from the file. “This isn’t a demand letter. She filed a formal complaint in Superior Court. It’s already public.”

“She wants headlines,” Bianca says. “She will get some. Then we will shut it down.”

“Has Blackwood been briefed?”

“He asked for you.”

That gives me pause. “He knows me?”

"He has read about you. He liked how you handled the Emory cross. Said you were surgical."

I am not sure if that is praise or a warning. "Is there merit to her claims?"

Bianca exhales, her gaze fixed on the Westwood skyline. Trent has a history of relationships with young women. Some have come after his money. The firm has handled more than one 'misunderstanding' for him in the past. He's very generous. And he believes in keeping things quiet." Her voice lowers to almost a whisper. "If Savannah succeeds, Ben, others will follow."

In the short time since the LA lawyers joined the firm, I'd heard the rumors about Bianca's rise, the whispers about her ruthless charm and the way she cultivated relationships with Blackwood and others. When I finally spent time with her, I wondered how she attracted a billionaire client.

Her words now, pragmatic and cold, settled the question.

"The investigator pulled social media metadata and text strings. It will not kill her case. But it will wound it just enough to win in court."

"Does Blackwood know we are going that route?"

"He knows to stay quiet and let you do your job."

Blackwood's LA office sits above Mulholland, all glass and clean lines. A private elevator takes me up. When the doors open, I walk into what looks like the lobby of a high-end hotel: mid-century furniture, a cold-pressed juice bar, and three assistants who look like they were recruited from a modeling agency.

He walks out a moment later. He doesn't reach to shake my hand. Instead, he grins at me.

"Ben Carlisle," he says, voice smooth and practiced. "The lawyer, Bianca says destroys witnesses in the courtroom."

He is in his fifties but dresses like he's much younger. He's wearing a tailored blazer, no tie, top two buttons open. I cannot tell if he is performing or if this is who he really is.

"I read your bio on the firm's website," he says as we sit. "Bianca says I am lucky to have you."

"I'm not interested in headlines," he says. "I expect victories."

"Same," I reply.

"Look, everyone in this industry knows how it works," he adds, waving a hand. "You play hard, you work hard, and sometimes you cross over the line. Especially when it comes to keeping the numbers looking good for the markets."

He pauses, watching me. Then adds, almost like a confession:

"You think investors want to hear we're settling another lawsuit? The second you admit risk, they start questioning valuation."

He leans back. "Savannah knew what she was doing. She instigated the whole thing."

"Did you sexually harass her?"

"No," he says, quick and dismissive. "She initiated it and it was all consensual."

I don't blink. "Did you ever text anything or do anything you would not want a jury to see?"

His smile fades. "Define would not want."

"I shot video of us having sex. I wouldn't want the jury to see that. Savannah wouldn't either. She put on quite a show, and I'm pretty sure it'd make the national news if it plays in court."

Blackwood is worse than I had expected.

"You still have the video?"

"No, I destroyed it."

I leave that alone for now.

Back in my hotel, I meet with Rachel Wolfe, the LA associate Bianca assigned to help. She is sharp, focused, and has already flagged inconsistencies between Savannah's complaint and her social media.

"Savannah posted photos from Cannes the same week she claims she was emotionally shattered," Rachel says, tapping through screenshots. "Smiling. Tagging brands. And here—she captioned this one: 'Living my best life. Thanks, TB."

"Time-stamped?"

"Verified. We pulled the metadata."

I nod. "Print it all. Back it up."

"I don't like going after her character," I say. "But I don't get to choose what's already been put in motion."

She pauses. "She was not a victim, Ben. She knew exactly what she was doing. She gave him what he wanted and made sure he would remember it. Now she wants to monetize the memory."

I keep my expression flat.

"Bianca has handled Blackwood cases like this before," Rachel says. "Robinson is not the first woman to go after Blackwood for his money.

I nod slowly. "And the NDA?"

"Enforceable. But only if we take the fight to her."

Bianca calls that evening.

"You saw the complaint," she says.

"I did."

"Then you understand the problem."

She exhales. I can hear movement on her end, the soft hum of her office.

"Savannah knew what kind of man Trent is," Bianca says. "He doesn't hide it. He can be seduced. She knew that."

She pauses.

"And she knew how to keep his attention."

I say nothing.

"This isn't about sex, Ben," she continues. "It's about money."

The line goes quiet for a beat.

"Come by the office tomorrow morning," she says. "I want to walk through the rest of it in person."

I am back in her Wilshire office the next morning. Bianca unlocks a drawer and hands me a thin manila envelope marked CONFIDENTIAL.

She hesitates, then slides a separate printout across the table. "There's one thing that doesn't make sense. Savannah was wired $2.5 million six weeks before she filed. It came from a shell LLC called Delano Capital Partners. No website. No employees. Registered to a PO box in Nevada."

I raise an eyebrow. "Was it part of her employment package?"

"No. There's no record of it in the HR file. Not even a non-disclosure agreement tied to it."

I say nothing, but the number sticks. You don't wire someone $2.5 million to stay quiet and forget to get it in writing. Unless you're trying to bury something that matters more than the money, that number smells like someone paid to erase a story before it started.

Bianca closes the file. "You saw that number. Someone paid her to disappear. You really think this is about sex and headlines?"

I'm sure it will make headlines, but I don't respond.

"We are going to destroy her," Bianca says.

Robinson's lawyer is Don Lansing. He's one of the leading sexual harassment lawyers in California. He represented dozens of women in cases against athletes, actors, and wealthy businessmen. He's represented other women in cases against Blackwood.

I know of him because, typically, before he files a lawsuit against someone famous, he goes on television with his client to announce the lawsuit and seek publicity. Before he filed the Robinson lawsuit against Blackwood, he had held a press conference that was played on every national news network that night.

Before the deposition goes on the record, Lansing leans in.

"If you come after her reputation, we'll come after your client's tech empire," he says quietly. "That's not a threat, Mr. Carlisle. That's a promise."

Savannah is dressed for sympathy. Soft pastels. Oversized sleeves. Delicate jewelry. Her makeup is flawless. Her eyes stay fixed on the court reporter more than on me.

At trial, I expect the jury will see her vulnerability.

I let her talk.

Then I start asking questions.

By the end of the deposition she has contradicted herself three times. She admits deleting text messages. Rachel's timeline memo forces her into a corner she cannot escape.

But Lansing does not blink.

"We'll see you at trial," he says.

Three months later, we are in a Los Angeles courtroom.

Savannah testifies for two full days.

She repeats the story from the complaint. The private jet flights. The Napa night. The pressure. The humiliation.

The jury listens carefully.

When it is my turn, I stand slowly.

"Ms. Robinson," I begin, "you testified that you were emotionally devastated after the Napa incident."

"Yes."

I walk to the screen and bring up the first exhibit.

A photograph from Cannes.

Savannah on a yacht. Champagne glass in hand. Smiling.

"Do you recognize this photo?"

She hesitates.

"Yes."

"You posted it on your Instagram account, correct?"

"I did."

"The same week you claim you were emotionally shattered?"

Lansing objects.

The judge overrules him.

Savannah shifts in the chair.

"I was trying to move forward."

I move to the next exhibit.

A text message.

Savannah to Blackwood.

Miss you already.

The courtroom is quiet now.

"Did you send this message?"

"Yes."

"That was three days after the Napa incident."

Her voice drops.

"Yes."

I continue.

By the time I sit down, Savannah has admitted she deleted messages, stayed in the relationship, and continued negotiating her compensation package.

When the verdict comes back a week later, the foreperson does not hesitate.

"On the claim of sexual harassment, we find for the defendant."

Blackwood exhales loudly beside me.

The reporters rush out of the courtroom.

Another headline.

Another scandal that disappears.

It's a win, but not one I am proud of. That night I sit in my hotel room staring at the exhibits spread across the table.

Rachel's timeline memo.

The metadata.

The deleted texts that somehow resurfaced.

Bianca's investigator deserves most of the credit. He found things no ordinary discovery request would have uncovered.

Too much, maybe.

I flip through the file again and stop at the wire transfer.

Delano Capital Partners.

Two point five million dollars.

Six weeks before Savannah filed the lawsuit.

Blackwood swore he never paid her a dime before trial.

Which means someone else did.

You do not wire someone that kind of money unless you are trying to solve a problem.

Or create one.

The jury believed our story.

But something about the evidence still bothers me.

I cannot explain how Bianca's investigator found half of it.

And I am not sure I want to know.

Bianca texts me later that night.

Just four words.

See you in Aspen.

I stare at the message for a moment before setting the phone down.

The case is over.

The jury believed us.

Blackwood is celebrating somewhere in the Hollywood Hills.

And Bianca is already moving on to the next victory.

But I keep thinking about that wire transfer.

Someone paid Savannah Robinson before she ever filed the lawsuit.

Which means someone knew this story was coming long before it reached the courtroom.

And whoever that was is still out there.

Chapter 7
The Summit

In sports, it's the scrimmage that decides who gets the ball when it really counts. In law, it works the same way. The real game is played in the quiet moments. Who gets invited? Who is watching? Who leaves with whom? That's where the next power shift begins.

I step off the gondola and onto the platform. The air smells like pine from the Aspen trees. Hamilton Reed rented the entire mountain.

Ten days earlier, a new email had landed at the top of my inbox.

Subject line: Partner Retreat – Aspen.

Evan's name was at the bottom, but Bianca had mentioned it first. The firm had secured The Summit above Aspen Mountain for an exclusive partners-only retreat. Three nights. Late summer. High-altitude strategy sessions. Client bonding. Celebration.

Spouses were not invited.

Top clients were.

Now, stepping off the gondola, I'm seeing firsthand how the firm is changing.

Holding a retreat here is our way of announcing we've arrived.

But I am no longer sure what that means.

String lights stretch across the deck. Fire pits flicker at the edges. A quartet plays something that sounds like Mozart until you recognize it is Coldplay. Champagne flows in every direction. The firm is staying at the most luxurious resort in Aspen, but tonight this mountaintop is the center of gravity.

A waiter hands me a glass of Dom Pérignon. He doesn't ask for my name. He knows it.

I stay at the edge for a while, watching. Partners from Dallas, Houston, Austin, San Antonio, San Francisco, and Los Angeles form their own clusters. The West Coast lawyers carry themselves like celebrities. Most of the Dallas group is overdressed and already over-drinking. Their laughter grows louder as glasses empty. Everyone is performing.

I spot Preston Locke by a fire pit, sipping from a heavy tumbler.

He nods to me once, and I nod back. We haven't spoken since I won the Robinson case, but I know what the victory meant. That's why I'm standing here.

Bianca Rivers walks through the crowd like she owns the mountaintop and everyone on it. Her white dress catches the light and holds it. The neckline plunges so low it draws attention. The slit along her leg dares you to look twice, but she never looks to see if anyone noticed.

I catch the scent before she reaches me. Tom Ford Soleil Blanc. She wore it at the bar. Tonight, it's stronger, or maybe I'm more aware of it. That was deliberate. Nothing she does is accidental.

She brought Paragon's CEO with her. He's wearing a midnight blue jacket, no socks, and polished loafers. His grin says this whole weekend was his idea. I've met him twice; both times, he acted like it was the first.

Someone calls for quiet, and a microphone clicks on.

Charles McAllister's voice slides through the speakers like he's managing a merger. "If I could have your attention."

The crowd settles. Only the wind keeps moving.

"Tonight is a celebration," McAllister says. "This year has exceeded expectations. We added ten Fortune 500 clients. We won every case we tried. We opened our California offices. And along the way, the top legal journal wrote that we are the fastest-growing law firm in the United States. That is quite something."

He turns toward me. I already know what's coming.

"One lawyer has made our firm famous. It's Ben Carlisle."

I don't move at first. The applause comes fast. A few voices call my name. I catch Preston's smile. Even Bianca claps, slow and cool.

I walk to the stage. I don't rush it.

McAllister slaps my shoulder and leans into the mic. "In the Blackwood case, the other side never saw it coming. Ben dismantled Savannah Robinson's claims with surgical precision, and the jury returned exactly the verdict it should have. The win made headlines across LA and reminded everyone what this firm can do in a courtroom."

Laughter breaks out, and the applause swells again.

I take the mic.

"Thank you," I say. "I'll keep this short. I know there's bourbon and something sweet waiting." That draws a few more laughs.

"Litigation is a team sport. And the best teams are built on trust. I trusted my team, and we got it done. That's what we do at Hamilton Reed."

That's all I give them. It's enough.

As I step down, the music starts again. The applause fades into conversation. Servers pass with trays of oysters and skewers of something I can't pronounce.

Preston finds me near the edge of the deck. "You looked comfortable up there."

"I was thinking about bourbon."

He chuckles. "You're being watched. That's both the good news and the warning."

"I figured."

He nods once. "That's a setup. Watch for the bait."

"I've seen bait before. The trick is knowing when not to bite. Anyone in particular?"

Preston doesn't answer. He tips his glass in Bianca's direction.

She's now leaning in toward Harvey Nichols, the litigation partner from San Francisco. Her hand brushes his lapel as she laughs. His eyes don't leave her face. She catches me watching and doesn't look away.

Out by the second fire pit, Evan Marston has had too much to drink. His voice carries even over the music. He's talking too loudly to Sienna Parker, one of the younger partners from Los Angeles. She shifts her weight and laughs politely, but Marston doesn't take the hint. He leans in closer. Sienna backs up slightly, keeping the line between awkward and uncomfortable. Marston sloshes his drink. Someone calls his name from behind, giving Sienna the out.

Preston sees it too. He says nothing. He turns back to the bourbon.

Around us, the flirting grows more obvious. Hands linger longer. Eyes stay locked a few seconds too long.

Bianca appears at my side without announcing herself. I do not notice until her hand rests lightly on my elbow.

"You look bored," she says quietly. "Want some company?"

I do not answer right away. The scent of her perfume is familiar now, deliberate. She knows I have noticed.

"I was watching the room," I say. "Who talks to whom. Who avoids whom."

Her smile flickers with interest.

"Careful," she says. "You start studying people like that, you may learn more than you want to know."

I meet her eyes and hold them before easing my arm away from her hand.

"That depends," I say. "On whether the truth is useful."

She studies me for a moment, deciding whether I am warning her or flirting with her.

Then the smile returns, slower this time.

“Be careful, Ben,” she says softly. “Curiosity has ruined better lawyers than you.”

“Maybe,” I say. “But it also wins cases.”

For a moment neither of us moves.

Then she turns and disappears back into the crowd.

The music swells and the party keeps going.

I stay where I am.

By midnight, the cigar tent is full. Someone starts a game involving tequila shots and bets on first-year billings. I step outside. I need air.

I stand at the edge of the deck and look out at the lights far below. Aspen glows in the valley. For a moment, I forget what this is. I forget the politics and let myself enjoy the view.

Then the wind shifts. Behind me, someone laughs too loud. Another voice tells someone else to keep it quiet.

I stay outside longer than I mean to. Things quiet down as I step away from the music.

Inside the cigar tent, the volume has doubled. Someone turns on music, louder than it should be. A few junior partners start dancing near the back corner. I recognize Ari Vaughn from San

Francisco. He's spinning a woman I don't know in four-inch heels and a silk dress. She's not with the firm. She may be with Paragon. At this point, no one seems to care.

When I step back in, I smell bourbon and perfume. Bianca is seated near the center of the room, surrounded by a small group. Harvey Nichols is still beside her. So is Evan. She's saying something about an upcoming panel she's moderating in Los Angeles, but I don't think anyone is listening to her words. They're watching the way she says them. She knows it.

She sees me walk past. Her eyes lock with mine. I keep moving.

In a corner near the bar, I find McAllister again. He's now hanging on the arm of one of the newer Dallas partners, Julia Carr. Julia looks like she's trying to manage the moment without creating a scene. I admire her restraint. McAllister keeps talking about a patent client in Houston. Then something that doesn't sound like work at all. Julia shifts again. He tries to put a hand on her back.

I make a decision and walk over.

"Charles," I say, friendly but direct. "Locke is asking for you by the fire. He says you owe him a drink."

McAllister blinks at me. For a moment, I'm not sure he can stand.

"You sure?" he asks.

"Positive."

He looks at Julia, then at me. "We'll continue this later," he says with a wink that makes her jaw tighten.

As he shuffles away, I turn to her. "You good?"

"Fine," she says. "But thanks."

I nod and leave it at that. She disappears into the crowd. I lose sight of McAllister somewhere near the deck doors. Hopefully, someone cuts him off soon.

Back near the center of the tent, Bianca stands. Her group follows, pulled into her orbit like it's inevitable. I watch as she makes her way through the crowd without touching a single body, yet every head turns. Evan says something to her. Bianca laughs, but it's a polished sound, the kind that means nothing. When she turns toward the exit, her hand grazes Harvey's shoulder. He follows.

Bianca does not look back. She does not need to. When she reaches the doors, Foster opens one without hesitation. Harvey slows, unsure whether to follow. Bianca keeps moving, and Foster follows.

I step out again, this time into night. The sky is ink black, and the town lights below are distant and blurred. Somewhere out there is the version of me who used to think being a lawyer meant a briefcase and a courtroom.

That version never imagined retreats like this, or what they might reveal.

A door opens behind me. It's Preston. He lights a cigar and stands beside me.

"They get any wilder in there?" he asks.

"Getting close."

He nods. "I remember when the biggest drama at these retreats was whether the fish was overcooked."

"It's not the fish anymore."

"No," he says. "It's who ends up in which room by morning."

He takes a long drag from the cigar, then glances over.

"You handled McAllister well."

"Someone had to step in. I figured it was better than waiting for HR to clean it up next week."

Preston grunts. "That's leadership. It's a rare thing lately."

He doesn't say more, and I don't press. We both know the firm is changing. Some of the people inside think this couldn't be better.

From the look on their faces and the huddled conversations, I'd say the old guard doesn't like it.

A few more partners spill onto the deck, laughing too loudly. One of them, in high heels, trips on the stairs and catches herself on the railing. A junior litigator from Houston is trying to impress someone from Los Angeles with a story about cross-examining an oil company witness. It sounds made up.

Preston finishes his cigar and puts it out neatly in a glass ashtray.

"I'm heading back down," he says. "Before more of our lawyers make fools of themselves."

I nod. "I'll stay for a while."

He starts toward the gondola, then stops. "If you see things, Ben, try to salvage the situation."

Then he's gone.

I lean against the railing and watch the lights flicker in the distance. The partners behind me are still drinking. Their voices are sharper now, and their flirtation has gotten more serious.

I finally decide to take the gondola down and go to bed.

The sun is too bright the next morning. That's the first thing I notice.

I sit up in bed. My throat is dry, and my head reminds me that I had more than one glass of bourbon after the speech. I reach for the bottle of water on the nightstand, down half of it, and then check my phone.

A text message from Julia Carr.

Julia says thank you. Nothing more.

Downstairs, the lobby is quiet but uneasy. Some partners are already checked out. Others drift through with sunglasses and black coffee. The hotel staff is too cheerful. That's how you know this place is expensive. They know how to act when rich guests act like jerks.

I spot Evan hunched over a breakfast table with someone from Paragon. He looks like he barely slept. I pass without stopping.

In the elevator, two Los Angeles partners are whispering about what happened on the gondola ride down. I hear the name McAllister. They're laughing about how he made a fool of himself.

The doors open. Neither of them looks at me.

I find coffee at the lounge near the spa and sit at the edge of the terrace with a view of the mountain, now scrubbed of last night's glamour.

A few minutes later Preston joins me.

"You stayed later than I did," he says. "Did McAllister finally call it a night?"

"Not exactly."

Preston raises an eyebrow.

"He tried to follow Julia to her room," I say. "Hotel security stepped in before he made it down the hall."

Preston exhales slowly. "That bad?"

"Worse if they decide to report it."

"Did they call the firm?"

"Not while I was there."

"Is he still here?"

"First shuttle out this morning," I say. "Hungover and angry."

Preston shakes his head. "Humiliation usually teaches people something. I doubt it will teach him."

We sit quietly for a moment.

I stir my coffee and think about the way McAllister slurred Julia's name. The way she kept smiling through it, refusing to let the scene belong to him.

"There will be consequences," Preston says. "Even if this stays quiet."

"And if it doesn't?"

"Then there will be more."

He studies me for a moment.

"Bianca was seen leaving with Harvey."

"I noticed."

"She wants power. He wants relevance."

"Bad combination."

Preston nods. "They both know the firm is changing."

"Into what?"

He leans back in his chair.

"That's the question."

He finishes his coffee and stands.

"See you Monday."

I stay on the terrace long after he leaves.

When I finally board the limo to go back to the airport, Bianca jumps in the back seat with me. She's wearing sunglasses. She doesn't acknowledge last night. She doesn't need to.

"You left early last night."

I don't respond.

We pull away, and Aspen shrinks behind us. We leave the mountain, but we're not the same firm that came up it.

I won the case that got me the spotlight here. But I'm starting to wonder what kind of price comes with the invitation. Because no matter how high we climb, something always waits below.

Chapter 8
The Victory Lap

In sports, the most dangerous moment comes right after a big play, when everyone celebrates and someone relaxes. That is when games turn.

In law, it's no different. The second you think momentum is yours, you stop looking for what might take it away.

#

The elevator doors open on the fifty-first floor. The office sounds normal, until it doesn't. Secretaries are huddled around a desk, whispering. When they see me, the conversation stops. Tessa brings coffee without being asked, setting it down with a smile I haven't seen before.

"Nice to have you back," she says.

"Good to be back," I say, though I am not entirely sure I mean it.

The office has a different energy this morning. In addition to the gathering of secretaries, I hear someone laughing in the kitchen. I check the hallway. Charles McAllister's door is shut.

A few hours later, I see Evan's and Bianca's names on an invite that hits my inbox.

Litigation team meeting: 2:00 p.m. Central with Video in all offices. Preston Locke will chair from Dallas.

Shortly before two o'clock, I finish what I was doing and head toward the conference room. I know that look. It means I'm becoming useful. Usefulness has its price, but I'd rather earn my place than wait to be noticed.

On the way, I pass two associates whom I don't know well. I think they are third-year associates. They straighten up as I approach, one of them giving me a quick nod, the other pretending not to notice me at all.

The conference room is already half-full. I take a seat halfway down the table. Preston is in his usual spot near the front, flipping through a legal pad. He looks as if he has not yet fully recovered from the retreat. Someone cues the video feed. A large screen at the head of the room flickers, then sharpens.

Lawyers from each of our offices appear on the screen. In LA, Evan appears first, framed by a floor-to-ceiling window with the Los Angeles skyline behind him. Bianca sits beside him, dressed in black, holding a clear glass like a prop. Even on camera, she looks striking. The dress fits like it was made for that chair. She doesn't speak. She doesn't need to. Her expression gives away nothing. I doubt that's accidental. Neither looks like they were on a mountaintop forty-eight hours ago. They look like they never left work.

Evan clears his throat. "Appreciate everyone jumping on," he says, voice tight with caffeine and confidence. "We are riding momentum right now. Big wins. New matters. Fortune 100 clients who are finally calling us first, not second."

He glances sideways at Bianca, who smiles slightly but says nothing.

"We need to stay sharp," Evan continues. "Ben's victory the Robinson case last month made headlines. Our Aspen celebration shows we are moving up fast. This is the time to double down."

He rattles off new assignments. A major IP case in Northern California. A cross-border dispute out of Mexico City for the San Antonio office. Six associates are being pulled onto a major document review for Paragon, and Bianca will coordinate that directly. She does not look at the camera, but I know her eyes are moving. Nothing about her suggests the weekend left a mark, which tells me more than anything she could have said. She listens closely, but not passively. It comes across as judgment, and no one wants to be on the wrong side of it.

"Final note," Evan says, "Dallas and Houston will co-lead the next general counsel summit. Preston, I will have you from Dallas and Ty McGrady from Houston coordinate that with our other offices."

The screen freezes for a beat, then returns. Preston thanks him. The meeting breaks quickly after that. Partners in Dallas file out, buzzing. Preston stays behind with two other partners. I head back to my office.

I've barely sat down when an email lands in my inbox. There's no subject line. Only a link.

The sender is one of the Dallas associates. I click the link.

It leads to a post on a site I've never seen before. It's called Greedy Associates. I quickly see that associates posting on it are using fake names to vent about billable hours and firm dinners. One thread catches my eye.

Golden Firm, Rotting Core?

Posted at 9:14 a.m. with already hundreds of comments.

I read.

The author claims to be a third-year associate in a Dallas law firm. Maybe the writer is a third-year associate, and maybe not. The writing is sharp. It's funny in a bitter way. The writer calls the Aspen retreat "a big-dollar celebration for lawyers who talk firm culture while drinking Dom Pérignon." Evan is called "the Emperor of Echo." Bianca is "Aspen's White Queen."

I can picture the nickname. Her hair is perfect. Her glass is empty.

Then I see it. Someone copied my entire speech.

I stare at the screen. Whoever wrote this didn't paraphrase. They had the full text. That means someone had a printed copy or an email with the remarks. Somehow, it ended up outside the circle.

The post continues:

"Litigation is a team sport," said the firm's golden boys as the lights twinkled over the mountaintop.

No mention of the 2,200 hours associates were expected to bill to stay employed. No mention of why the firm spent more on the retreat than on training last year. What mattered was the message, not the math.

I forward it to Preston.

Seen this?

He replies in less than a minute.

Yes.

That is all. He makes no comments about the post.

I read it again. Someone on the inside has an axe to grind and access to documents that should have been protected. That means most likely a Dallas partner leaked the documents to an associate.

I close the tab and glance at my closed door. Then I pull the post and scroll down faster this time. The final lines cut deeper than I expect.

"This place teaches you to smile, to work your ass off, and to win at all costs. But some of us are starting to ask how much money the partners are making off of our hard work."

I don't know who wrote it, but I know he or she doesn't like the firm, and they want to convey to associates and law students that Hamilton Reed is a sweatshop.

A knock interrupts the thought.

It's Julia Carr.

She steps in without waiting and closes the door softly behind her.

"Did you see it?" she asks.

I nod.

She sits across from me, with no pretense this time.

"It was on my phone before I even finished reading the morning email."

"Are people talking?"

"They are pretending not to. But yes."

We sit without speaking for a moment. I wait to see if she is going to bring up McAllister. She doesn't.

"What do you think happens next?" she asks.

"Nothing," I say.

She nods. "But someone will check it out."

"Of course."

"Any guesses?"

I shake my head.

Julia stands. Her voice drops a level.

"They quoted you, Ben. Word for word."

I know that is not a good thing.

She opens the door, then looks back.

"I did not send it. And I did not write it. But it is not wrong."

She leaves.

I sit there for a while, not touching the keyboard, not looking at the screen.

Later, I walk down the hall to Preston's office. His assistant isn't at her desk outside the office. I knock once and step in.

He waves me in without looking up. A legal pad and a draft memo are spread across his desk. He gestures to the chair.

"You read the whole thing?" I ask.

"Yes."

"You know who gave the information to the associate who wrote it?"

"No. But I have a list."

He leans back. Eyes me carefully.

"You are not on it."

"I wouldn't blame you if I were."

Preston half smiles. "You're ambitious, but you're not careless. And you are still loyal."

"To what?"

He shrugs. "That is the real question now."

He stands, walks to the window, and looks out at the skyline. He does not say anything for a while.

"I have seen this before," he says finally. "Not what the young lawyer posted, but the belief that partners are making a ton of money off their billing 2200 hours or more."

"They're making ten times more than I made starting out."

"I think they are less interested in the money and more interested in work-life balance."

"I get it, but there's no such thing as work-life balance in a law firm. I worked seven days a week, sometimes twelve hours a day, getting ready for the Robinson case that we won."

"I know. They don't care about you."

"What do we do?"

He turns. "Keep working and keep an eye out for anything unusual, especially anything unusual from the LA lawyers."

I nod and leave.

By five o'clock, the tone of my floor has shifted. Phones are still ringing and I'm still receiving emails, but the conversations are shorter. The easy rhythm of the days following the firm retreat has given way to something more controlled. Even Tessa seems to sense it. When she drops by, she asks if I want her to check with IT about anything odd on my calendar.

"No," I say. "Not yet."

A memo comes out from Firm Communications. It reads like any other internal announcement. It's a reminder to avoid nonsecure devices when working remotely. A few polite words about digital hygiene. A note that printed materials should be properly shredded.

It does not mention the post.

But the timing is not subtle.

Someone sends around a redacted copy of my Aspen remarks. It matches the language I used almost exactly. The message is clear. Control the narrative. Bianca's name isn't on the memo, but the tone matches her style. It's polite, precise, and written so cleanly that no one would dare argue with it.

Late in the day, when I'm ready to go home, I open a client file I'd been ignoring. The spreadsheet makes less sense the longer I look at it. I think about the person who wrote the post. I wonder what pushed them. Was it Aspen? Or was it because doors stayed shut between meetings?

I close the file.

The laughter down the hall dies too quickly. A door slams harder than it should.

From the outside, the Dallas office looks the same.

Inside, the firm has changed.

And none of us can pretend otherwise.

Chapter 9
The Suite Life

In football, some games are won before the first play.

It happens in the owners' offices, in backrooms, and at dinners where futures are traded in toasts and favors. By the time the players take the field, the outcome is already in motion.

Likewise, in law, some cases are won before the first juror is impaneled. They're won by what investigators uncover about the opponent and what they pass on to the trial lawyers.

The tension in the Dallas office doesn't break, but it changes. It settles into something quieter, masked by closed-door meetings, deadlines, and client calls. For a few days, everyone acts as if things are normal. Then Bianca proposes a change of scenery. She calls it a team-building weekend. It's a celebration, she says. But it's about optics. The Cowboys game weekend is her idea.

She pitches it to Evan and me like it is some kind of strategic corporate retreat, a bonding exercise. "Team building," she calls it, flashing the smile that promises more than it delivers. Evan, ever the agreeable one when it comes to a good time, signs off on spending the money instantly. It's a firm expense, after all.

My job is to handle the logistics. Dallas is my city. Hamilton Reed might have offices elsewhere, but the firm's roots, and my roots, are here. I call The Mansion on Turtle Creek and secure a block of suites for the entire group. They are the highest end, of course, the kind of place where even the air feels expensive. I book one suite for Erin and me, another for Cassidy Knox, and four more suites for the LA contingent. Bianca and Evan each get their own. Blackwood gets one for himself and Summer Vance. Rachel Wolfe gets the fourth. This is Hamilton Reed, and we don't do things by halves.

They're a high-wattage bunch: Bianca and Evan from LA leadership, Rachel Wolfe, the junior associate who helped me win the Robinson v. Blackwood case, Trent Blackwood himself, and his model girlfriend, Summer Vance. Cassidy and Erin round out the Dallas side.

Saturday afternoon, they descend. The Mansion's discreet valet whisks away their black Escalades, and I meet them in the opulent lobby. The space, usually a serene haven, instantly buzzes with a different kind of energy. Bianca walks in without breaking stride. The room shifts. Conversations pause, then resume louder than before. White pants, black top, heels that change the geometry of the floor. She doesn't slow to see who's noticed.

Erin elbows me to get my attention. "Try not to trip over your jaw," she murmurs. I smile, but I'm already watching Bianca work the room.

Evan walks in like the weekend was his idea, not Bianca's. Flashy watch, untucked shirt, white linen pants, designer sneakers. He plays the role well. Always has. But underneath the charm is a lawyer who never makes a move without an angle.

Trent Blackwood, Bianca's billionaire client, doesn't need to be overtly charismatic. His power hums beneath the surface, a quiet current that draws attention without trying. Summer Vance, the hottest California model, walks in beside him. She's impossibly tall, with a cascade of blonde hair, and an air of cool detachment that makes her presence even more striking.

And then there's Rachel, quiet as ever. She carries herself with a quiet intensity. She observes more than she speaks, a sharp contrast to the others. She nods to me, a flicker of something in her eyes I can't quite place. Erin and Cassidy are already there, exchanging polite but wary smiles with the LA crew. It's less like a Dallas weekend and more like an LA takeover, the grandeur of The Mansion suddenly feeling like a showcase for West Coast wealth and dominance.

That evening, the eight of us pile into a limo, destined for The French Room at The Adolphus, a Dallas institution, hushed and gilded, where the ceiling stretches high above polished floors and heavy chandeliers. It's the kind of place Hamilton Reed books when we want to impress, to signal our arrival at a certain echelon.

We slide into a large, semicircular banquette that seems better suited for an anniversary dinner than a firm celebration. The other patrons are mostly older, dressed like they've been coming here for decades. Our table draws attention. So does Bianca. She's already on her phone before the first course, quietly scanning for the most exclusive bar in Dallas to take the group after dinner. The French Room may speak to the firm's roots, but Bianca is only half-listening. She's planning the next scene.

She positions herself between Blackwood and me, subtly steering the conversation even when others speak. She leans in and laughs a shade louder than necessary, always aware of the angles.

Evan chats with Cassidy. Erin tries to draw Summer into conversation, but the model mostly gives polite, one-word answers, eyes drifting around the room like she's looking for an exit. Rachel, quiet as ever, sits across from me, listening more than talking. Her gaze flicks to Bianca now and then, but when Bianca starts mentioning new client revenue from the LA office, Rachel shoots me a look I can't quite read.

The wine flows freely, a deep ruby red that matches the room's plush decor. First, Premier Cru, then champagne for toasts. The conversation is a dizzying blend of self-congratulation, inside jokes about the Blackwood case, and veiled references to future deals.

After a few glasses, Blackwood becomes more talkative, sharing anecdotes about tech deals and power players, his voice a low, gravelly rumble that commands attention. Bianca punctuates his stories with sharp, witty remarks, her laughter ringing a little too bright. She leans into Blackwood again, arm brushing his in a way that makes it look natural, even with Summer Vance across the table.

As dessert plates are cleared and the check discreetly handled, Bianca slides her phone across the table to Evan. "Found it," she says. "Newest rooftop bar in Dallas. Private booths. DJ starts in thirty minutes." She looks around the table, eyes bright. "Let's not waste the night."

Evan nods, already texting the driver. Blackwood barely glances up before signaling his agreement. But when Bianca turns to Cassidy, Cassidy doesn't even pretend to smile. "I'll pass," she says. "One scene like this per night is enough."

Bianca shrugs like it doesn't matter, then turns to me. "You?"

"We're heading back to The Mansion," I say. "Long day tomorrow."

Bianca tilts her head, smile tight. "Suit yourself. Don't blame me when you miss the best part."

She rises, already moving, herding the ones who said yes like she always does. Erin doesn't say anything, but I feel her hand find mine as we watch them go.

****

Sunday morning dawns bright and deceptively fresh. The lingering scent of last night's excess clings faintly to my clothes, even after a shower in our suite at The Mansion.

We meet the LA contingent downstairs for brunch at The Mansion Restaurant, choosing the convenience of staying in-house over venturing out. The room is bright, elegant, with soft jazz drifting from a corner and sunlight streaming through tall windows. Despite the refined setting, the conversation feels brittle, still laced with the after-effects of the previous evening's indulgence.

Everyone orders mimosas or Bloody Marys, the hair-of-the-dog ritual a quiet acknowledgment of the night before. Blackwood, despite his late night, still manages a practiced charm, holding court over scrambled eggs and roasted potatoes. Bianca, too, seems unfazed, her energy levels unwavering, almost unnervingly so. Rachel sips her coffee, her expression unreadable.

By mid-morning, a fleet of black limousines waits outside The Mansion's stately entrance. Stepping into the cool leather interior feels like entering a private bubble, sealed off from the rest of Dallas.

The drive to AT&T Stadium is a blur of cityscapes giving way to sprawling parking lots.

The closer we get, the more chaotic the crowds become, a surging sea of blue and silver jerseys, tailgaters grilling and shouting. Our limo, however, bypasses the mayhem, granted special access. It glides effortlessly past security checkpoints that stop thousands of others. We are escorted directly to a private entrance, a testament to Hamilton Reed's influence, to the level of access money can buy.

Inside the stadium, we ride a private elevator up to the Hamilton Reed suite. The doors slide open to reveal a sprawling, glass-fronted space overlooking the field.

The suite is loaded with food and drinks. The staff circulates, ready to cater to every whim. This, I realize, is what "we've made it" really looks like.

The game itself is almost secondary. The Hamilton Reed suite becomes a revolving door of important-looking people, including local politicians, other prominent Dallas attorneys, and even a few former Cowboys players. Everyone wants to rub shoulders with Trent Blackwood. Everyone wants to make a connection.

"You think Dallas can top LA?" Evan jokes, clinking his glass with mine.

He grins, but I know him well enough to hear the edge behind it. He's not talking about skyline or barbecue. It's all about money. He's saying LA lawyers bring in more money than we do. He's probably right. He's all about the money, so I know why he'd like to make that point in front of our Dallas clients.

The drinks flow even more freely here than they did at dinner. Champagne flutes are constantly refilled, top-shelf liquor pours steadily into crystal tumblers. The air is thick with laughter, shouted conversations over the roar of the crowd, and the clinking of glasses. It's a performance, a loud, relentless affirmation of success. We're part of it, expected to play our roles.

Bianca works the room without circling it. She's never far from Blackwood, but never attached. When she speaks to him, others lean in to hear. When she laughs, it ends the moment it needs to. Summer Vance fades into the background without Bianca acknowledging her at all.

Erin's irritation is a tangible thing. I catch her watching Bianca and Blackwood, her lips pressed into a thin line. Later, when Bianca corners me to offer a dazzling compliment about "handling Dallas," it's not the words that throw me. It's the timing. The way her eyes linger, like she's already imagining the next move.

Erin's eyes are on us. She doesn't say a word, but I know what she is thinking. I try to brush it off, flattered despite myself, but the unease stays. Bianca's attention isn't about appreciation. It's a calculation. Flirt to throw me off balance. Let Erin see it. Remind everyone who really runs the room.

Rachel Wolfe is the quietest of the group. She watches, like Erin, but her gaze holds a different kind of intensity. She's not irritated; she's analytical, taking everything in. I see her talking briefly with Cassidy, a quick, hushed exchange before Bianca's laugh pulls everyone's attention back to her and Blackwood. The game unfolds on the field, a blur of motion and distant cheers. The real action isn't on the field. It's playing out here in the suite.

As the fourth quarter winds down, the group begins to thin. The celebratory mood, fueled by hours of heavy drinking, has begun to curdle into exhaustion for some, a lingering high for others. Finally, with the Cowboys securing a comfortable win, it's time for departures.

The Los Angeles contingent piles back into their limos, headed for DFW. Blackwood waves dismissively from inside his vehicle, Summer Vance a silent silhouette beside him. Evan offers a perfunctory handshake. Bianca, however, pauses. She gives me a bright, dismissive smile, then her gaze sweeps over Erin and Cassidy. "See you all soon," she calls out, her voice still strong, already moving away.

But Rachel Wolfe doesn't get into the limo with them. She stands beside me as the others drive away, the cold Dallas air cutting through the remnants of the suite's warmth.

"I'm staying here tonight," she says, her voice low. "I booked a room at the Magnolia Hotel near the office." She doesn't elaborate. I nod once. I want to hear whatever she plans to tell me.

Cassidy and Erin's limo pulls up. I nod to Rachel, a silent acknowledgment of her unexpected decision. Inside the limo, the moment the door closes, the dam breaks.

Cassidy is first. “She’s a vulture, Ben. Hanging on Blackwood like he’s her ticket to relevance.”

Erin follows, sharper than I expected. “She wasn’t selling the firm,” Erin says. “She was showing Blackwood who mattered in that room. You looked like you forgot I was sitting right next to you.”

I'm exhausted, the alcohol buzzing in my head. I try to dismiss it, "It's Bianca being Bianca. She's always been like that." But even as I say it, I know she’s right. I saw it too, the way she cozied up to Blackwood, and the way he responded.

We finally get home. The house is quiet and cold. Erin kicks off her shoes. “Never again,” she says. I nod, too tired to argue. "No more Cowboys games. Not with them." I tell her we’ll never spend another weekend entertaining LA lawyers and their clients.

My phone buzzes. A text from an unknown number. I open it.

Can we talk in the morning? Need to meet. Urgent.

It's Rachel Wolfe.

Chapter 10
The Metrics Shift

Every team reaches a moment when the safe play won't save the game. Someone has to break the script, take the tough shot, risk the blame.

Law is no different. Most stay silent to protect themselves, but the few who speak up risk everything.

#

I'm back at the office before dawn on Monday.

About thirty minutes later, Tessa walks in, holding my coffee mug and her reading glasses. She doesn't say anything until I take the mug.

"You didn't sleep."

It's not a question.

"It was a long day at the Cowboys game. Entertaining the LA crowd."

She nods slowly. "You've got that look again. Like you wish you'd stayed home and not spent the day with them."

"A Cowboys game with clients is an all-day affair. It starts with brunch and ends when everyone's drunk enough to forget how they got home."

Tessa doesn't press. Instead, she lifts her coffee cup and disappears outside my office.

At 9:00 a.m., I see Rachel Wolfe at my door.

"Do you have a minute?" she asks.

I nod, already sensing I won't like what comes next.

Rachel closes my door behind her, but doesn't sit. She opens her bag and pulls out a thin manila folder.

Rachel slides the file across the desk.

"This was buried in a directory that gets wiped every quarter," she says.

I scan the pages.

Therapist. Prescriptions. Ex-boyfriend.

"Who authorized this?"

Rachel points to the signature.

Bianca Rivers.

I look up.

"Why are you showing me this?"

Rachel hesitates.

"Because it isn't just the Robinson case."

She glances toward the door.

"I can't explain the rest here."

"Then where?"

"Lunch. Somewhere away from the office."

Rachel turns to leave and says, "Be careful, Ben. Once you know, you can't not know. And this is not the only one. Can we go to lunch somewhere private? There's more to the story I need to tell you."

I agree. Three hours later, she's back at my office. We walk several blocks to one of my favorite spots for lunch meetings. It's quiet. Soft jazz plays in the background. I lead Rachel to a booth in the back, the one furthest from other diners.

She sits across from me and sets her phone on the table but doesn't look at it.

"Thanks for meeting me," she says.

"You asked for privacy," I reply. "You have it."

Rachel stirs her iced tea without drinking it. Her usual composure is gone.

"I shouldn't be saying this," she says finally. "But I'm scared. And I think you're the only one who might listen."

I wait.

She glances around even though the room is nearly empty.

"It's about the firm," she says. "About what's really going on."

"What do you mean?"

"I worked at Marwood Shaw five years before the merger. I thought I knew how things worked." She shakes her head slightly. "I didn't."

I stay quiet.

"At first it was just comments," she says. "Suggestions that certain partners expect more than good work. That if you want to stay on the big cases, especially the celebrity ones, you need to be… available."

Her eyes stay on the table.

"Are you saying someone came onto you?"

"Not directly. Nothing you could prove. That's the point."

She finally looks up.

"But when I started keeping notes, I found something else."

"What?"

Rachel leans forward.

"I reviewed settlement memos from three harassment cases," she says. "The women all dropped their claims before trial. The billing entries were almost identical. 'Private resolution.' 'Confidential terms under counsel direction.'"

She pauses.

"One included time billed for something called 'third-party reputation management.' Another listed a 'background rehabilitation specialist.'"

I frown. "I've never heard of that."

"Neither had I."

She slides a small stack of documents across the table.

"I think Bianca is using investigators to dig up leverage," she says. "Personal history. Medical records. Anything they can use to pressure these women to walk away before the press gets involved."

"Not Robinson," I say.

Rachel shakes her head. "No. That one went to trial. But the others ended quietly."

Her voice tightens.

"And the litigators weren't told how the information was obtained."

I study the pages.

"You're saying the firm paid for all of this."

"I'm saying someone did," Rachel replies.

She sits back.

"I used to admire Bianca," she adds. "Now I'm not sure I know who she is."

For a moment neither of us speaks.

"You're the only person I could tell," she says quietly. "You're not part of them yet."

"And you think I might do something about it?"

"I hope so."

When lunch ends, she leaves in an Uber headed for DFW.

She looks calmer as the car pulls away.

I'm not.

Back in my office, I'm struck by the hours Rachel spent digging and the risk she took telling me. I try to dismiss it, but I can't.

I keep seeing Rachel's face when she said they would ruin her. From the way she looked when she said it, I'm worried they'll ruin me, too.

Sleep doesn't come. By the time the city is still dark, I'm back in my office. The halls are empty. I want a few minutes of privacy.

I pull up the firm's internal billing entries. The codes are vague. The descriptions even more vague. I see entries for private resolution meetings and client satisfaction sessions.

Cassidy's old warning pushes in: You don't even see it.

Maybe I didn't. Maybe I didn't want to.

The silence of the empty office amplifies everything. Rachel said no. They isolated her. I see it now, between the lines.

If anyone ever looks at this, the billing alone raises red flags. Bianca misused firm funds. She was behind the coerced settlements, and my victory in the Robinson case. But the feds won't stop with Bianca. I'd be in their crosshairs.

Movement in my doorway breaks the focus.

Cassidy Knox appears, holding a coffee mug and scanning the room like she's taking inventory. She doesn't smile.

"You're in early," she says. Her voice is calm, but not casual. "Working on something?"

I keep my face steady. “Clearing out some files.”

She nods once. Not buying it, but not pushing either. Cassidy never plays dumb, and she never asks twice unless she wants you on record.

She steps inside and sets the mug down on the corner of my desk. “I’ve seen that look before.”

Cassidy studies me for a long second. “Be sure whatever you’re chasing is worth the risk.”

That lands harder than any threat would. She isn’t warning me off because she’s part of it. She’s warning me because she’s seen what happens to people who try to take it on alone.

I hold her gaze. “I don’t know what you think I’m doing.”

She doesn’t blink. “You’ve already made up your mind. Be sure you’re right about who to trust.”

She leaves her coffee behind and walks out the door. I’m left with the knowledge that someone in this office sees more than she lets on.

I stare at my phone. Rachel’s words won’t leave me: You are not one of them. Not yet. Cassidy’s warning presses just as hard. They did not invite you to dinner. They asked for your commitment.

I should let it all go. It isn't my fight. I don't even know if Rachel really trusts me. But I know what I saw. The records. The coded billing.

Rachel didn't come to me by chance. She's not a panicker. She's deliberate. And whatever she uncovered is real. Something she couldn't ignore, and now I can't either.

Helping her will make enemies, especially the Los Angeles partners. Staying quiet will make me one of them.

The decision should be simple. It's not.

I think about Rachel across from me at lunch. The way she twisted her hands. The way her voice dipped when she said no. How quickly they isolated her.

It comes down to that. Rachel said no when partners started harassing her. Now they're punishing her.

I leave for home. Before I start my car, I pick up the phone. My thumb hovers.

She trusted me. She's the only one who did.

I send the message. It's short. Clear.

I'm in.

The words flash delivered. That fast, it's real.

At 6:30, I walk inside my home, and Erin is standing at the kitchen island with a martini in hand that she made for me.

"Monkey 47 Gin," she says. "Your favorite. Straight up with an olive."

I smile while picking up the glass, then sit in my recliner and quietly drink the martini.

Suddenly, Erin's voice cuts through the silence.

"Ben? You okay?"

I turn toward her, caught.

"Yeah," I lie. "I'm still tired from our long day entertaining the LA crowd."

She nods and turns to me again, hesitating like she wants to press but thinks better of it. "You're not usually so quiet when you get home."

I force a smile. "Big meeting tomorrow. I've got to get my mind on it."

Erin turns one more time. "Then after you finish drinking, let's have dinner, watch a little TV, and get a good night's sleep."

"Sounds good," I say. But as she leaves for the kitchen, I know it won't be a good night's sleep.

When Erin leaves the room, I sit alone, slowly drinking the gin, lost in thought. Rachel's face drifts into my mind again, equal parts fearful and relieved.

I lean back and stare at the ceiling. I know the fallout is coming. The LA partners will know Rachel told me about the Blackwood case. McAllister will eventually figure it out. I'm on Rachel's side now, whether I like it or not.

When I walk into the office tomorrow, I'll act like nothing's changed. But I'll know better.

Chapter 11
The Day Everything Changed Forever

They tell you to always stay ready, but nothing prepares you for when your number gets called in overtime with the season on the line. Suddenly, you're not watching anymore. You're the one who will win or lose the game.

Law is no different. One moment, you are on the sidelines. The next time you are in the middle of a fight with everything at stake and no time to think.

#

I'm in my office before dawn, before anyone sees me.

I try to focus on work. But my mind stays in Los Angeles. On the choices the LA lawyers made and the ones I didn't stop. My name's on one of the filings. That's enough to get pulled in, whether I like it or not.

My door stays closed. The only sound is the hum of the building coming alive. I stare at the phone, waiting.

It lights up.

One message. Then another. Then more.

I read the first twice. Then the second. Then the third. Each one hits harder than the last.

Rachel was right. They're coming after the firm.

DOJ subpoenas. Official investigation. LA is under fire.

I thought I could stay above this. Watch without being part of it.

That was naïve.

There's no watching from the sidelines anymore.

I push back from the desk and stand fast. My chair hits the wall behind me. I pace, rubbing the back of my neck as more messages pour in.

Tessa appears in the doorway, holding a printout and a cup of coffee. She doesn't walk in.

"You're walking around like something's coming," she says. "Should I be worried?"

I don't answer.

She takes one step closer. "Whatever you're thinking about doing, remember who you were before this place made you forget."

She sets the paper on the side table and disappears down the hall. No drama. No follow-up.

Another message comes in.

IMMEDIATE ACTION REQUIRED.

Then another.

DOJ DEMANDS — DEADLINE 4 PM.

A third.

URGENT — CALL ME NOW.

It's happening too fast.

I cross to the window and yank the blinds open. The sky is still dark, but softening at the edges. The world is moving forward while everything here is collapsing.

One line in the email catches my eye:

A request for all drafts of SEC responses and internal revisions to investor disclosures.

That's not routine. That's targeted.

They don't just want the final language. They want intent.

I glance back at my desk. Notes. Records. Printouts.

Yesterday's admin is today's evidence.

Brooke's voice echoes in my head. *You're doing great. Don't mess that up.*

I told myself I could handle her. Stay close without getting pulled in.

She didn't pull me under.

I walked right in.

That wasn't encouragement. It was a dare. And I took it.

Rachel's warning cuts through next. *Ben, you're not one of them.*

She knew. She took the risk.

Last night, so did I.

Two words.

I'm in.

Too simple. Too final.

My phone vibrates again. Voicemails stack up.

"Ben, you seeing this? This is serious."

"Call me back."

"Do not ignore this."

Then Bianca.

Her usual cool confidence is gone. In its place is something sharp and panicked.

"Carlisle," she says. Behind her, phones ring and voices shout. Chaos bleeds through the line.

"I just saw the news," I say.

"This is a goddamn overreach," she snaps. "They're twisting everything. Calling an aggressive strategy fraud. Since when is that illegal?"

She barely pauses.

"We protected our client's reputation. That's our job. And now they're throwing around words like suppression and coordinated takedowns like we're criminals."

Her voice tightens.

"They're flooding the zone with subpoenas. Dragging our SEC filings into this like we misled regulators. We cleaned up language. Every firm does that. It's chaos here, Ben. And it's getting worse."

"It's everywhere," I say.

"Who's handling this for Dallas?" she demands. "We're getting hammered. You have no idea how bad this is."

She turns away from the phone, snaps orders at someone nearby, then comes back blunt.

"The Feds are in here taking boxes. Client files."

"I'm getting details," I say. Even to me, it sounds hollow.

"You need to get back to me. Now."

The line goes dead.

I lower the phone slowly.

The edits were not cosmetic. They removed warnings that might have spooked investors, including references to litigation risk and pending investigations.

Those are the kinds of disclosures companies are required by law to make.

Leaving them out misleads the market.

That is securities fraud.

I think back to the Blackwood lawsuit. Robinson took it all the way to trial, and the jury ruled for Blackwood. But the damage had already been done. Once the complaint was filed, the allegations were everywhere. Investors do not wait for verdicts before reacting.

With Bianca directing the defense, the case eventually collapsed in court. But long before that happened, the pressure was already building. Posts disappeared. Statements were withdrawn. Non-disclosure agreements were signed.

Rachel flagged one of the edits last quarter. Bianca wanted to remove a line about litigation reserves.

I approved it without giving it a second thought.

Now I wonder if that moment was the beginning of something much bigger.

Neutral is over.

The fire is spreading. And I'm already in it.

The TV flips on. Red banners crawl across the screen.

SUBPOENAS ISSUED TO LOS ANGELES LAW FIRM.

I turn up the volume.

The words repeat. Louder each time.

Investigation. Bribery. Obstruction of justice. Concealment.

Partners drift in. Faces tight. Steps cautious. No one speaks.

A news chopper circles a glass building. Agents carry boxes marked **EVIDENCE**.

Phones ring. No one answers.

Then Preston Locke steps in.

He doesn't speak at first. He stands near the door, arms crossed. His presence steadies the room. Younger partners glance his way, waiting for something that will make sense of this.

"Dallas had visibility on some of those SEC filings," he says. Not accusing. Not softening it either. "Someone here approved them."

His eyes sweep the room.

Then they stop on me.

He doesn't nod. He doesn't smile.

He waits.

This isn't just about money to him. It never was.

The LA office appears on screen. The sleek headquarters Marston and Rivers paraded during merger talks.

Seeing it raided feels unreal.

Bianca's Arthur Andersen comparison chills me. Most people remember the name, not the outcome.

The firm collapsed under federal charges tied to Enron. By the time the Supreme Court reversed the conviction, it didn't matter.

The damage was done.

That's what scares her.

Phones buzz again.

No one moves.

"The Department of Justice is investigating allegations of conspiracy to obstruct justice and abuse of civil litigation in connection with the firm's representation of tech billionaire Trent Blackwood."

The anchor's voice stays calm.

The words cut deep.

Partner's shift. Some lean forward. Others lean away.

Bianca's name flashes on my phone again. I let it ring twice before answering.

"Did you hear what they're saying?" she asks.

"Blackwood," I say.

"This didn't happen until Dallas got involved," she says.

She doesn't say my name. She doesn't have to.

"You need to fix this."

"I'll call you back."

I won't. Not soon.

Another voicemail. An associate, voice shaking.

"They're asking about shredders. Late-night document runs…"

LA sees this as our fault.

They see me as the spark.

On screen, agents load boxes into black SUVs. Reporters crowd the sidewalk.

Locke ends a call and sets his phone down hard.

"This will settle down," he says.

He doesn't believe it.

Brooke speaks next, calm as ever. "They're making it sound bigger than it is."

She isn't worried.

She's watching us. Watching me.

Calculating.

The room holds its breath.

Locke breaks the silence.

"You see what's happening, right?"

He moves to the table and drops the merger memo down.

"I've been saying this from the start."

No one challenges him.

"They're calling it legal warfare," he says. "Weaponized defamation. Coordinated suppression. That's not just unethical. It's criminal."

His eyes lock on mine.

"We need to draw a line now. Before the Feds draw it for us."

"Once DOJ starts talking obstruction," he adds quietly, "an indictment isn't far behind."

He's right.

They didn't just defend Blackwood. They filed suits based on false claims. Sealed pleadings to keep the press out.

The DOJ sees obstruction, fraud, conspiracy.

They're right.

Cassidy speaks. "That's our play?"

I meet her eyes. "That's the only play."

"And if the rumors are true," Preston adds.

The room waits.

I have to decide whether I stay and help rebuild this place or leave before it collapses.

The offers sit in my inbox.

The chaos has burned itself out, leaving something unexpected behind.

Clarity.

Leaving would be easy.

Staying feels right.

Not because I owe the firm anything. I haven't been here long enough for that.

But if I walk now, McAllister decides what this becomes.

That's not the story I want Claire to hear one day.

I want her to know that when things fall apart, you don't run.

You rebuild.

By late afternoon, the partners gather in the conference room.

They're quieter now. Focused.

I don't waste time.

"We need to move fast," I say. "LA is gone. We don't save them. We save ourselves."

No one pushes back.

"Clean separation. Today."

Some of them wonder if I'm the one Dallas will sacrifice.

If I'll cooperate.

I don't address it. Not yet.

The room shifts.

Not hopeful. But steady.

When the meeting ends, no one rushes out.

Then my phone buzzes.

Rachel.

"They let me go," she says. Calm. Too calm.

"When?"

"An hour ago. Restructuring. NDA attached."

"How much?"

"Enough to disappear."

I don't answer.

"They think I'll sign and forget I submitted the SEC responses," she says. "The final ones. After you said the edits looked good."

She doesn't ask what to do.

"They're cleaning house, Ben. Sooner or later, they'll come for you."

Maybe.

But I'm not backing off.

The line goes dead.

I stare at the desk.

The stakes just changed.

And whatever I do next, Claire will know exactly what kind of lawyer her father is.

So will everyone else.

Chapter 12
No Turning Back

In sports, not every attack is direct. Sometimes the opponent slows the game, cuts off your angles, and forces you to wait. Mistakes don't come from pressure. They come from the silence in between. Law works the same way. You're not pushed out. You're just left out until you start questioning everything.

#

Over the next few weeks, I'm piecing together where things stand.

A former client texts me late at night: "*Did you really sign off on surveillance? Thought you were better than that.*"

I don't reply. I don't even know what he's talking about. But it's out there. The LA team may have used private investigators and likely hired someone to follow Savannah. I don't have proof, only rumors, and it's out there now.

DOJ is investigating obstruction and fraud. Rachel showed me documents tying the LA team to Blackwood's response strategy. Lawsuits built on claims they couldn't prove. Evidence buried.

NDAs used to end the cases quietly. And when DOJ started asking questions, documents disappeared.

On top of that, I hear rumors about parties involving LA partners and young women from the firm. Enough stories, told the same way, to make me believe them.

I'm not getting calls now. LA partners are quiet. Dallas partners become polite, then distant. The urgency fades. It's replaced by something colder.

Brooke steps back. Not all at once, but enough to notice. Some meetings happen without me. Some invites go quiet. She doesn't lead the charge. But she doesn't stop it either.

I've done nothing wrong, but some of my partners believe I might be indicted for my work on the Blackwood case. Spending time with me might draw fire.

Preston Locke still stops by my office. Late one afternoon, he appears in the doorway and leans quietly against the frame. He says nothing. He doesn't need to. His presence says he's not joining the freeze.

"You hanging in?" he asks.

I nod. He doesn't push. He stays a moment longer, then moves on. It's a small gesture, but I hold on to it.

Moments like that are rare now. That afternoon, Bianca calls. Her voice is surprisingly composed and calm. She assures me that she and the LA partners have everything under control and tells me not to worry if the feds come calling. I want to ask how they could possibly have it under control if the feds are knocking, but before I can, she hangs up.

Later, I sit alone in my office. I think about how quickly Brooke distanced herself. It doesn't surprise me. It's almost like she planned it, knowing exactly when and how to pull back. I hear other partners mention my name, their tones cautious like they expect the feds to come after Dallas because of me.

Even the associates who used to hang around when the LA merger landed have started to steer clear.

I catch glimpses in the hallway. Conversations pause when I pass. They aren't hostile towards me. It's more like everyone's waiting to see where the DOJ investigation goes.

Then Eric Fontaine shows up at my door, casual in a way that isn't. He pauses in the doorway, asks how things are going, and waits. I've used the same move myself. He used to bring jokes. Now he brings questions.

"Everything cool?" he asks. "You've been under the radar." His tone is easy, too friendly.

"Staying out of the crossfire," I say. "Unless there's a meeting I wasn't invited to."

He offers a dry smile. "Everyone's reassessing priorities right now."

"Sure," I say. "And I'm guessing Brooke's helping with the reassessment."

He shifts, just slightly. "Everyone's saying we should wait and see." The words aren't his.

He doesn't stay long. He doesn't need to. The message is clear.

Brooke is the director behind this. I hear her voice carry through the hallway. "Should we really be backing off?" she says, loud enough for others to hear. She's making sure people repeat it.

Later, she talks to Russell Briggs, a well-respected Dallas litigation partner, who started with the firm out of SMU law school and has been here for over thirty years. "Do you think Ben needs help?" she asks, glancing in my direction.

She knows exactly what she's doing. The associates follow her lead. Now, when they look at me, it's not because they're curious. They're deciding what to do next. One whispers, "It's bad," as I round the corner.

I tell myself the isolation won't last. But I know better. A younger partner asks Briggs, "Things will shake out, right?" He waits. Briggs doesn't answer.

I see it clearly. LA is dragging Dallas into the mess. Brooke made sure of that.

McAllister doesn't speak to me.

She's playing for keeps.

They know what this is. So do I.

It's evening, and I try to focus. I keep my head down and stay at my desk, acting like the whispers haven't reached me. Brooke senses it. She doesn't back off. Another partner stops by. I've spent so little time with him since I joined the firm that I don't even remember his name. "Ben," he says, as if that's enough. "Everything OK?"

I give a brief nod and return to my screen. No follow-up. He leaves satisfied. I assume he's on his way back to Brooke's office to report.

They keep coming one by one. They sound so rehearsed. Brooke's fingerprints are on every pause, every glance, every question disguised as support. It spreads. Meetings happen without me. Emails slow to a trickle. Partners avoid eye contact. Associates steer wide in the hallway.

I keep my head down and work through the silence.

When I leave the office, I pass a bar two blocks away. Through the window, I spot Brooke, Eric Fontaine, and three other Dallas partners laughing and raising their glasses. I watch from across the street. I tell myself it doesn't matter, but I know it does. Let them have their drinks. I'll still be here tomorrow.

The next morning, Fontaine stops me by the elevator. "You should have come last night. Brooke ordered your usual."

I look at him. "Must've gotten lost in the invite shuffle."

"Funny how that happens," he says, grinning like we both know exactly what's going on.

No one reaches out for days and then weeks. Brooke doesn't need to say anything. Her plan is in motion. Let me isolate. Let me twist. If I fall, they survive. That's her plan.

Each day, I sit at my desk and focus on my work. It's better than thinking about the firm and realizing that I might be the one they sacrifice. And better than wondering what Claire would think if this ends with her father's name in the press.

I tell myself it won’t last. That someone will break. That the pressure will turn. But deep down, I know Brooke is only getting started.

And the silence won’t hold forever. Something bigger is coming. I know it. The first sign hits with an email from the general counsel of a long-standing client.

I call him right away. "The message surprised me," I say, keeping my tone level.

"Just want to be sure you're still solid," he replies. His voice sounds rehearsed. "Lots of news."

I hear the real message buried under the polite concern. Brooke’s narrative had already reached him.

"We have an important case, but I’ve been told to take it elsewhere," he adds, every word deliberate and with no hesitation.

A week ago, this conversation wouldn’t have existed. We had history. Trust. That’s gone. Doubt replaced it.

I push back, pointing to our track record, but he’s already moved on. He tells me he’s been directed to take the case to one of my competitors.

"We'll be back once the dust settles," he says. "I may be able to convince my CEO to come back to you." We both know that's not likely to happen.

After he hangs up, the hit stays with me, not because of what he said, but what he didn't. He asked no real questions. Offered no support. He withdrew.

By late afternoon, more client emails land. All carry the same cautious tone: *Is everything okay over there?*

One GC adds a note I can't overlook: "*We've heard troubling things. Not just from DOJ, but in the press. Hope they're not true*."

Nothing has been published yet, but the story is already taking shape. Someone is feeding it to the press.

What started in LA is now impacting us in Dallas. And my name is tied to it.

Not hearing from other clients troubles me. They haven't officially left the firm. But I know they're abandoning me soon.

The message hits before sunrise.

SUBPOENA DUCES TECUM

UNITED STATES DEPARTMENT OF JUSTICE

You are hereby commanded to produce all documents, records, communications, and electronically stored information, including but not limited to emails, internal memoranda, time entries, billing records, and meeting notes, pertaining to your professional activities and communications with attorneys, staff, and clients associated with the Los Angeles office of Hamilton Reed LLP, including but not limited to work performed on behalf of any clients originating from or managed by said office, from January 1, 2023, to the present.

Production shall include all personal and firm devices or accounts used to conduct Hamilton Reed business or communicate with the Los Angeles office, whether official or informal in nature.

Failure to comply may result in penalties under federal law, including but not limited to obstruction of justice.

They want everything, and they're working their way towards me.

"Failure to comply may result in… charges of obstruction."

I forward it to the firm's general counsel. Then I sit back, thinking about options.

If I refuse, they'll prosecute me. If I cooperate, I'll risk taking the firm down with me.

Brooke's campaign boxed me in, but DOJ finishes the job. They want both documents and my testimony.

The deadline blinks from the screen.

I'm in the crosshairs.

Rachel warned me. Brooke warned me in her own way. I underestimated them both.

I sit in front of the screen, knowing I have to act.

There's no safe play left. No easy out.

For a moment, I consider ignoring it. Then I read it again.

I lean forward, hands tight on the desk.

This goes beyond protecting the firm.

It's about protecting myself. And making sure no one rewrites what really happened.

I stay late, waiting for the office to empty. No one stops by. No knock at the door. No quiet reassurances.

I thought at least one of my partners would say what they're all thinking. But their silence says enough.

I'm being shut out. They think I'm going down with LA, and they're keeping their distance.

I could lie low. Let things cool off.

But I won't.

Not when they're rewriting the story without me in the room.

Ten minutes later, Tessa steps in with a file I didn't ask for. She sets it on the desk, then lingers just long enough to make it clear she didn't come in only to deliver paper.

"Can I say something?" she asks, voice even.

I nod, still staring at the screen.

"You look like a man deciding between two bad options," she says. "There's always another move. You have to look where they don't want you to."

She doesn't wait for a response. She turns to leave, then pauses at the door.

"Don't let people like Brooke or Bianca decide who you are," she says. "That was never part of the deal."

Then she's gone. The door clicks shut behind her. And for a moment, I consider calling her back—but I don't need more words.

I already know she's right.

Later, the heels come first. I know who it is from the sound before I see her.

Bianca.

She enters without knocking, already in control. Cream silk blouse, dark tailored slacks, everything about her effortless and exact. She wears the same perfume. Light, expensive, familiar. She moves closer, and the scent pulls me back, reminding me how often I underestimated her.

“You’re brave to show up here.”

“Bravery has nothing to do with it. I clean up my messes. Or at least redirect them.”

Without asking, she slides onto the edge of my desk. Casual but too close. A move that says she belongs. A move that says I do not.

"Am I interrupting?"

She knows she is. She didn’t come only to talk. Her expression gives that away. So does her timing.

I can’t tell if she came to warn me, recruit me, or frame me.

Before she says anything else, I speak.

“What the hell were you thinking? Don’t pretend it was only about Savannah,” I say. “You made sure this didn’t trace back to the firm, didn’t you? Is that how the firm handles billionaires who prey on young women?”

She tilts her head like she expected the question. Maybe even wanted it. But she does not answer.

"You left me hanging while you pulled the strings. Now the Feds are coming for the firm, for you, and maybe for me, too.

She pauses long enough to make me wonder if she will answer at all. Then she composes herself again, calm as ever.

“You’re still on the inside, Ben,” she says, her voice smooth, legs crossed. “But keep pushing like this, and you’ll lose that. And once you’re out, no one will protect you.”

“If DOJ finds the settlement NDAs, the investigator reports, or the instructions to delete those emails, it’s over for everyone.”

Bianca doesn’t flinch.

“Then make sure there’s nothing left to find.”

I study her face. She is not worried about the Robinson case. That one went to trial, and the jury ruled for Blackwood. The verdict is public record.

But the work that led up to that trial is another matter.

Bianca and her investigator dug into Savannah Robinson’s life before the case ever reached a courtroom. They found enough to give me ammunition on cross-examination, and the jury watched her credibility collapse piece by piece.

If this explodes, Bianca will make sure the story is that I directed the investigation into Robinson and approved whatever methods were used to dig up that evidence.

"Think it over," she says. "I'm not flying back until tomorrow. Join me for drinks after work. A few partners will be there."

She doesn't wait for my answer. If I show up, that will be the answer.

She leaves. The scent of her perfume lingers after she's gone.

The door clicks shut. The room is quiet again.

But the warning stays with me.

You're still on the inside.

Now that I know she is willing to lie and claim I orchestrated the Robinson investigation, this is no longer about right and wrong.

It's about control.

The drinks invitation isn't social.

It's a test.

If I show up, I stand with them.

If I don't, she knows exactly where I stand.

Either way, Bianca writes the story.

The only question is whether I'm part of it.

Chapter 13

The Test

In sports, the biggest plays sometimes happen before the whistle. A look, a bump, a quiet comment. They want to see if you'll react. Show weakness and they keep coming. Show control, and they back off. Law works the same way. Not every test is public. Some happen in private moments when the room is watching to see if you flinch.

#

Lawyers and staff leave around me. I remain at my desk. By six the floor is quiet. By seven the hallway outside my office is empty.

The partners from Los Angeles are already at the bar downstairs. Bianca made sure I knew where.

If I don't go.

Bianca will notice.

So will the others.

Skipping drinks won't prove anything, but it will tell them something has changed.

My name is already on some of the filings.

If this turns into an investigation, that will be enough to pull me in.

I lean back and stare at the ceiling. I decide it's better to know what they're planning than to be dragged in blind when the DOJ starts filing charges.

I grab my jacket.

Bianca stands in the center of the lounge, surrounded by the LA team and a few Dallas partners who showed up. Their voices rise when she speaks. The others gather around her.

I stand at the edge long enough to remind them I'm not leaving quietly. Then I step in.

When they spot me, they look surprised for a moment. Bianca lifts her glass, eyes cool and unreadable. Her fingers tighten slightly around the stem. I can't tell if she came to warn me, recruit me, or frame me.

I order a drink and pretend to be relaxed. The glass gives my hands something to do.

They act like my place here is already decided. I catch the looks. A pause before someone answers me. A glance toward Bianca before a comment lands.

Someone jokes about “long weeks ahead.” Another says things are “sorting themselves out” quickly. No one says my name.

“Things are calmer now,” one of Brooke’s people says, staring straight at me. “No need to panic.”

Texas has been silenced, and they want me to hear it out loud.

I expected this. But hearing it cuts deeper than I thought.

Evan joins in. “Thought you would bail.” His grin is slow and deliberate.

They want to see if I’ll beg or slip up. I don’t give them the satisfaction.

“Just like Dallas to be cautious,” Evan says.

I don’t respond. Nothing I could say would change anything.

Bianca leans in, voice soft. “See how easy this can be.”

Her smile does not reach her eyes.

I stay longer than I planned. Leaving would mean they won.

Bianca is mid-sentence when her phone lights up.

She glances down, frowns, steps away.

She answers low at first, then her voice sharpens. “Wait. What?”

Laughter fades. Conversations stall. Heads turn.

"No. Who authorized that? No one notified us," she snaps.

She strides to the back, still on the call. The others murmur. Brooke's crew watches. Even Evan stops smiling.

Eric Fontaine checks his phone. His face pales.

"Jesus. It's real," he mutters.

"What's real?" I ask.

"FBI. Los Angeles office. They walked in with warrants. Right now."

Phones come out. Voices rise.

Bianca reappears, face tight. "They're in the building. Agents. Taking everything."

Brooke is unreachable. Partners retreat behind closed doors. Some leave fast, already calling lawyers.

Bianca meets my eyes across the room. The charm is gone. She looks trapped.

I step toward the exit.

Tonight was supposed to be my test. Now it's theirs.

The lights are low when I return. The office is empty except for the cleaning crew's vacuums.

I head straight to the conference room and spread the documents across the table: billing records, internal emails, memos Rachel handed me before everything unraveled.

The originals were shredded in Los Angeles. If they went that far with hard copies, someone scrubbed the digital trail as well.

Whatever was in these pages, they wanted it gone.

For weeks, I tried to stay out of it. Tonight ends that.

I sort quickly. Coded billing for hours never worked. Notes on skirting disclosure rules. A cryptic reference to "sensitive leverage strategy."

Then it clicks. Evan and Bianca were fabricating grounds for lawsuits to silence women who could accuse Blackwood of harassment. Blackwood had the money. They helped him weaponize the system.

This was deliberate.

I told myself I wasn't part of it. I was wrong.

I group the documents: Brooke. Bianca. The LA partners.

They think I'll stay silent to protect myself.

If I hand any documents over, the LA lawyers will say it was me who hired the investigators. If I cooperate, they'll pin the cover-up on me. If I refuse, the feds indict me and they'll say the same.

I dial Kip Sutter.

"Kip. It's bad. I need you."

"Yeah. The whole city has." His voice is wary.

"It won't stop with LA. This is going firm-wide. I have files that need protection and review. Off the books."

Pause. "Ben, if you're asking me to do anything illegal—"

"I'm not. I want this handled clean. Your advice."

Another pause. "I'm listening."

I give him the broad strokes.

"I'll look," he says. "But if it turns, I walk."

"Fair."

I end the call and shut the cracked door.

They hung Dallas out to dry. Let me twist.

Not anymore.

Now I'll answer loud enough for everyone to hear.

Morning comes early.

I barely slept, replaying the files, the strategy, the veiled threats.

My phone buzzes with alerts before dawn.

DOJ Executes Surprise Raid on Hamilton Reed's Los Angeles Office

Fallout Spreads to Texas Office After Federal Action

Major Clients Question Future of Elite Firm

No spin. No control.

Texts pile up: clients, colleagues, old friends.

"Is Dallas part of this?"

"Ben, this doesn't look good."

By seven, I'm at the office. Phones ring nonstop. Tessa looks pale, clutching coffee.

"Nonstop since I got here."

I close my office door. The quiet lasts less than a minute.

The first client call: "This isn't personal, but we're suspending new work until this is sorted."

I understand. I hate it.

More calls, same message.

Later, Rachel calls.

"You seeing this?"

"I'm living it."

"They've cut off phones. Emails bounce. Brooke, Bianca, and Evan are locked in behind closed doors in LA."

I hang up. Across the room, the document boxes wait.

LA's silence is deafening. They think Dallas is isolated, me buried.

I grab my notepad and start drafting:

Clients to call back.

Partners to monitor.

Strategy to shield Dallas.

The LA lawyers want an easy target.

I won't be it.

The first calls go better than expected. A few clients agree to wait. Some sound reassured.

Then a junior partner steps in without knocking.

"You need to see this."

She shows me the headline:

BREAKING: DOJ sources confirm investigation could expand to Dallas if evidence of broader involvement emerges.

This isn't only about LA anymore.

It's Dallas. It's me.

They're coming.

I won't be caught flat-footed.

I reach for my phone. No hesitation.

Enough.

It's time to push back.

Chapter 14
The Firm Breaks

In sports, momentum swings fast. One minute, the home team controls the game, the next, a turnover shifts everything. The crowd quiets, confidence drains, and suddenly, the team chasing is the team in charge. Law is no different. Power can vanish in a moment, and when it does, the ones left standing are forced to decide whether to panic or play through.

#

After another restless night, I arrive at the office expecting tension held in check. Instead, it spills into the halls.

I walk toward the sound and find partners clustered around flat screens. No one greets me. They watch names scroll across the bottom.

The headline reads: **Hamilton Reed partners taken into custody.**

I see Bianca first, then Evan, and finally Blake Emory. The three of them are led out in cuffs. Bianca looks composed. Her expression stays unreadable. She moves as if she expected this.

No one in Dallas speaks. We all know what it means.

LA is in freefall. We could be next.

My partners look at me for answers. I have none.

Brooke's name is absent from the arrest list. I expected that. She always kept distance from Evan, Bianca, and Blake.

Before speculation can settle, an email lands from Brooke. She says she is cooperating to avoid prosecution. She tells us to focus on clients, who will soon question the firm's viability.

Some partners panic. They turn to me. I shrug. They scatter.

I walk the halls. Two partners I trusted talk openly about joining other firms. They do not lower their voices.

Junior lawyers gather in clusters, speaking the same way.

Three partners arrested on national television, accused of silencing victims and obstructing justice. It puts the entire firm in jeopardy.

I thought we could hold on. Now I am not sure.

As days pass, more partners leave. Many were here longer than me. Some joined right out of law school and never planned to go elsewhere.

By noon, my phone rings. A global firm wants to open in Dallas. They ask how many Hamilton Reed partners I can bring.

They want fifty or more. They care about the numbers, not me.

"Ben," the partner says, his voice polished. "We want to be in Dallas. Bring your team. Open our office and run it your way."

Minutes later, another firm calls with the same pitch.

For a moment, I picture it. Many partners would follow me.

The thought fades.

I do not answer more calls.

Then Preston Locke appears at my door.

He steps in, closes the door, and sits across from my desk.

"You really thinking about it?" he asks.

I do not answer. I know firms are calling him too.

"Richard Hamilton built this place," Locke says. "Fifty years ago, practicing law was a profession. Being part of this firm meant something."

I listen.

"I know McAllister changed that when he brought in LA. They have done us great harm. But don't be the one who finishes Richard Hamilton's firm."

He studies me. Locke does not bluff.

"We've been through worse," he adds. "You weren't here for the savings and loan scandal. It almost ended us. We came back."

He leans back. "We'll come back again."

I am not sure we will. But he believes it.

Locke's presence slows the panic. For the first time today, my breathing steadies.

"You're sure?" I ask.

"Sure enough," he says. "I've asked the Dallas partners to meet in the conference room. Come sit at the head table."

I nod.

Ten minutes later, we sit at the head table.

Partners arrive and fill the room without small talk. McAllister is not among them.

Locke stands. "LA is finished. We all know that."

No one argues.

"If we sit back, LA will take us down with it."

I rise. "Clients and lawyers are already leaving. Other firms want them."

Some partners nod. Others stare at the table.

"We cut LA loose, focus on Texas, and fully cooperate with the government," I say. "The SEC is circling. DOJ may not stop with three arrests."

Silence.

Then Cassidy asks, "That's our play?"

I meet her eyes. "That's the only play."

Partners exchange glances. Slowly, they nod.

"Cooperate and survive," Locke says.

They accept it.

After the meeting, I return to my office. It is dark. DOJ demands fill my screen.

I thought turning over everything would feel like betrayal.

It does not.

LA collapsed on its own. Partners and clients fled. The office closed. The damage was done before the rest of us knew what they were doing.

We are not surrendering. We are doing what we must to survive.

The demand is clear: *Failure to comply may result in obstruction charges.*

No wiggle room.

If I do not cooperate, the Texas offices die with LA. If I cooperate, we may survive.

I gather the records. Each file could save us or end us.

Headlines scroll.

Prosecution of Hamilton Reed's LA Office Threatens Dallas Stability.

Reporters say I stayed and cooperated to save the firm.

Why did I stay? Maybe I do not want to be the man who let Richard Hamilton's legacy burn.

That sounds noble. I am not sure it is true.

But for now, it is the reason I can live with.

Chapter 15
The Price of Truth

In every season, there comes a point when the game is no longer about winning. It is about surviving. The scoreboard does not matter anymore, whether you are up by ten or down by twenty. What matters is who stays on the floor when the shots stop falling and the crowd stops cheering. Law is no different. When the verdicts are in and the headlines fade, what matters is who stands beside you when there is nothing left to win but your own survival.

Our Dallas office still has people in it, but most doors stay closed. Conversations stop when I walk past. A partner who thanked me last week for helping save the firm now looks down at his phone.

They blame my work on the Blackwood case for how close we came to losing everything.

No one mentions my agreement to cooperate with the DOJ, but everyone knows I will hand over my files.

I check my inbox. Emails come from reporters, clients, and recruiters.

I stay at my desk for hours. Phones ring in offices and voices carry down the hall. No one stops by my door.

My phone lights up. Brooke calls.

Her cooperation is official. The feds have given her immunity for her testimony. By the time we hang up, headlines and alerts report the agreement.

I step into the hall. Several partners stand together.

“She’s naming names,” one says.

They do not say my name.

News spreads quickly. Brooke Chandler has agreed to testify in exchange for immunity.

I overhear another group. “Ben’s close to this,” one says, gesturing toward my office.

I text Brooke. She does not reply.

Outside my door, partners keep talking.

“How far will she go?”

“Will she protect Dallas?”

No one sounds confident.

TVs run nonstop in the break room. Clients forward articles to my phone. They want answers.

Brooke moved first to protect herself. I saw that coming.

I stand by Tessa's desk. A partner says, "She'll bury us if she has to."

They glance toward me. Tessa looks up.

I do not move. I do not react.

He is right, but I am not about to agree.

I nod at Tessa and return to my office.

Before I plan my next step, Preston Locke calls.

"Lunch," he says.

I meet him at a quiet restaurant on Field Street.

He sits at a table with two steaks already ordered.

"Sit down, Ben."

"You've done enough," he says. "You can leave it here if you want."

I stay quiet.

He cuts into his steak. "You held the line. You kept Dallas alive. You don't need to stay and deal with what's coming next."

He speaks directly. "Other firms would take you. You would start clean."

I listen.

"You stepped in when no one else did. You made the call that saved us. The others know it. But they won't forgive it either."

He leans in. "They are scared now. They will turn on whoever reminds them of the risk. Don't give them the chance."

I sip water.

"You and I have seen how loyalty gets punished."

I nod slowly. If I leave now, the firm can draw a clean line. I become the firewall.

"You are forty-four," he says. "You have time to build something better."

"You have already made up your mind about me," I say.

He shrugs. "I have seen men hold on too long."

He slides the check toward me and stands. He leaves without waiting for my answer.

I sit alone for a minute.

I pass Russell's office. The door stands open. Boxes stack near the desk.

I step inside. He packs files, books, photos.

"You look in a hurry," I say.

"Everyone is," he answers.

He tapes a box. "I never planned on leaving, but there is not much left to hold on to."

"You have been here your entire career."

He shrugs. "You did what leaders do. You made the hard call."

"I know the partners," he says. "They will come around."

"They did not take it well."

"They never do." He lifts a box. "You will be fine."

He carries the first box out. He does not look back.

Russell's office is empty when I walk past again. His nameplate is gone.

Emails from national firms arrive. They know what I could bring. They do not know how closely the DOJ still watches me.

I need distance.

I open a new message.

Subject: Stepping Away

"Effective immediately, I am stepping back from client matters. Please redirect all active files and communications to Cassidy Knox."

After reading the message once, I click send and stand, crossing the office to the window.

The graduation photo of Erin and me sits on the corner of my desk. I take it in my hand for a moment, then slide our daughter's note into my briefcase and add one book before closing the bag.

Client files stay on the shelf. Awards stay on the wall. I leave everything else in place. I am not clearing out. I only need distance.

I turn off the desk lamp and the overhead light.

No one asks where I am going.

I wait for the elevator. I step inside.

In the lobby, the security guard nods.

In the car, I place my briefcase on the passenger seat and start the engine.

I pull into the street.

At a red light, I glance in the rearview mirror. The building stands behind me. The windows are dark.

The light turns green. I drive forward.

Erin waits at home. She could say she warned me. She has not said it yet.

That says enough.

Chapter 16
Fractures Widen

#

There comes a point late in the game when the strategy shifts. You stop playing to score and start playing to avoid mistakes. Protect the lead. Manage the clock. Limit risks. Winning now means surviving the pressure without giving the opponent an opening.

Law is no different. When collapse threatens and the stakes rise, success is measured by who keeps steady and avoids costly moves. Staying in the game becomes the only goal. The ones who last are the ones who know when to stop pressing and start protecting.

#

I arrive home. Erin sits on the edge of the sofa. Her arms stay folded. The light beside her casts a soft glow across the room.

"You're home early." Her voice stays calm.

I set the cardboard box on the floor. It holds a few personal items from my office. "I needed space today," I say.

She studies my face. "Did you leave the firm?"

"No. I did not resign. But I am stepping back. The firm is in chaos. The DOJ investigation has everyone on edge. I had to get out of that building."

I take a few steps closer. She stays where she is.

"So you packed up and walked out?" she asks.

"I needed distance," I say. "Sitting in my office and pretending everything was fine stopped working."

She presses her lips together. "And bringing home a box changes that?"

"Not overnight," I say. "But it gives me room to think."

She exhales slowly. "I just want to know what this means for us."

"I haven't walked away from us," I say. "I'm trying to figure out what I'm going to do next."

She does not respond right away. Her eyes soften.

Finally, she asks, "What is your plan going forward?"

"I need clarity on what I face. Then I will decide what to do next. Whatever it is, I will not let anyone else decide how this ends for me."

The next morning, the doorbell rings.

A courier stands at the door with a sealed envelope from the United States District Court.

Grand jury. Los Angeles. Two weeks from today.

I call Michael Levin. We went to law school together. He practices criminal defense in Los Angeles now.

We finish small talk. I read him the heading.

"Not unexpected," he says. "They are casting a wide net."

"Am I going to be indicted?"

"Not necessarily. They want your testimony."

He advises a proffer agreement. We gather documents. Emails from Rachel. My notes. Billing records. One memo Rachel flagged months ago references "media risk containment." I include it.

A week later, news breaks. Local outlets first, then national. "Hamilton Reed Partner Subpoenaed" links to the investigation.

Colleagues avoid eye contact. Dallas law firms stop calling.

My phone buzzes. Bianca's name appears.

I answer.

"Ben," she says. Her voice stays smooth.

"Bianca."

"I heard about the subpoena."

"It was bound to happen."

"Perhaps. But how you respond matters now."

"I am consulting with my attorney."

A pause. Her tone shifts.

"Certain details tend to surface when people push too hard. Details that would destroy your credibility and Savannah's."

"What details?"

"It is better if you do not know."

I say, "I appreciate the concern."

"Good. Because once you burn bridges, you cannot repair them. Take care, Ben."

She ends the call.

I spend several days at Michael Levin's office in Los Angeles. We review every document, line by line. We anticipate questions.

Each night, I return to my hotel and review notes again.

By the morning of the meeting, I am ready.

I meet Michael outside the First Street U.S. Courthouse. We enter together, pass security, and reach a plain conference room. White walls. No windows. One long table.

Two assistant U.S. attorneys sit waiting. They motion for me to sit. Michael takes the chair beside me.

They open files. I answer questions. I stay within the proffer agreement.

One closes a folder and leans forward.

"Mr. Carlisle, we would like to discuss your involvement in the Savannah Robinson matter—specifically, your work for Trent Blackwood."

Michael answers. "My client cannot answer questions about his representation of Mr. Blackwood. Those communications are protected by attorney-client privilege."

A prosecutor straightens. "Your refusal could be interpreted as non-cooperation."

Michael says, "That is not a refusal. It is a statement of privilege."

The session continues with more tension. I answer carefully.

As it ends, they escort us out without a word.

Outside, the sun is bright. We walk to Michael's office in silence.

After a debrief, a driver takes me to LAX.

I return to Dallas.

My name now appears in headlines tied to the firm's collapse. Law firms no longer show interest.

At home, Erin and I talk less each night. One night, she says, "I do not know what we should do now, Ben. This uncertainty is tearing us apart."

I have trouble sleeping. I lie awake replaying choices and conversations with Bianca and Blackwood.

The next morning, a courier arrives again. This time, a subpoena to testify before the grand jury in Los Angeles. The letter states I am now a target.

I stare at the words.

I call Michael. "Come the day before to prepare," he says. "They are not offering a proffer."

"They asked about Blackwood last time," I say. "They pushed."

"You were right to refuse. You do not give that up unless a court orders it."

I fly to Los Angeles alone.

At LAX, I pull my suitcase to the waiting car. It takes me downtown to the hotel.

Michael and I meet that evening. We review everything again.

The next morning, we walk to the courthouse.

A clerk leads me through security to a narrow hallway. Michael waits outside.

He stands as I approach. "Do not volunteer. If they go near Blackwood, invoke privilege. Tell the truth, but do not speculate."

A door opens. "Mr. Carlisle. They are ready."

The room is small. The court reporter sits at one end. Prosecutors at another. Grand jurors face forward.

I take the oath.

The lead prosecutor introduces herself. "Mr, Carlisle, my name is Danielle Vaughn. I am an Assistant U.S. Attorney. You are under oath. Your answers are recorded. You may step out to confer with counsel."

"Yes," I say.

She opens a folder.

"You represented Trent Blackwood during key events under investigation. Correct?"

"Yes."

"Did Mr. Blackwood ask you to suppress evidence of his misconduct with Savannah Robinson?"

"That question calls for attorney-client privileged communications. I respectfully decline to answer."

She moves on. "Did you hire the private investigator who harassed Ms. Robinson?

"No, I did not hire a private investigator to harass Ms. Robinson. Rachel Wolfe later showed me documentation that a private investigator had been hired. One memo from Blackwood's publicist referenced hush money and deleted footage. Bianca had signed off."

"Did you attend meetings where destruction of records was discussed?"

"No."

"Were you aware files related to celebrity clients were removed from servers?"

"I became aware after Rachel Wolfe showed me documentation."

"Were you suspicious before that?"

"I would like to step out to confer with my attorney."

In the hallway, Michael listens.

"You can answer," he says. "You did not act on it. Stick to the timeline."

Back inside, I say, "I had concerns. But I did not have facts. Rachel's documents made the pattern clear."

Danielle Vaughn presses. "You continued recruiting clients. You kept cashing distributions. Were you profiting from misconduct?"

"No. I believed I was operating ethically."

Questions continue fast: timelines, emails, travel.

I step out twice more.

When they return to Blackwood, I invoke privilege again.

After two hours, Danielle Vaughn says I am free to go.

Michael meets me outside. "You held the line."

"Do you think I am still a target?"

"They have not told us different."

On the flight home, I replay the session.

An email arrives from the local bar association, requesting a meeting about allegations tied to my work for Blackwood.

A client calls. “My board is concerned. We have to put our relationship on hold.”

A recruiter calls. “The firm is hesitant now.”

At home, Erin asks if I want coffee. We sit without talking.

My phone rings. It’s Preston Locke.

“I heard you met with DOJ in LA.”

“I did.”

“It took courage.” After a pause, he says, “Dallas is reeling.”

We talk about the human cost. His support helps.

My resolve hardens. I will not violate privilege. I will face the consequences.

Chapter 17
The Bar Inquiry

In sports, sometimes you're on the field with the ball in your hands. Other times, you're in the locker room with the coaches replaying every snap, every missed assignment. In law, this is that moment. The whistle's already blown. The scoreboard's frozen. And now they're deciding whether I even deserve to keep practicing law.

#

The drive to Austin passes quietly. Greg Halston sits beside me. He defends lawyers in disciplinary matters from his Houston firm. He says little. He knows what this means. So do I.

We arrive. Greg walks in with me.

I adjust my tie. The receptionist gestures. "Mr. Carlisle? They are waiting for you."

I walk down the hall. The hallway smells of stale coffee.

She stops at a glass-walled conference room. Three people sit inside.

Thompson, the lead panelist, is a former appellate judge. I recognize him from arguments I made before him. His expression stays neutral.

"Mr. Carlisle," he says. "Thank you for coming. This is an inquiry, not a disciplinary hearing. What you say today may inform future proceedings."

I nod. The DOJ was looking for crimes. The Texas State Bar was deciding whether I could keep practicing law.

I scan the room. Marcus Kendrick sits on the panel. We opposed each other in a contract dispute years ago. It was long and messy. He nods at me. No warmth shows in his eyes.

A water pitcher sits in the center. Three glasses remain unused. Legal pads align neatly. A recorder waits.

Thompson clears his throat.

"Mr. Carlisle, when did you first suspect misconduct at Hamilton Reed?"

"My concerns arose in late 2023."

"And did you report them to anyone at the firm?" Ramirez asks.

"No. I did not have enough to discuss with anyone."

"Were you aware a private investigator had been retained in the Robinson matter?" Kendrick asks.

"I became aware after the trial."

Questions continue. They probe my knowledge and actions.

"Would you describe your relationship with Mr. Blackwood as typical attorney-client?"

"Yes."

They make notes. No one challenges me directly.

Caldwell leans forward. He is older, with white hair.

"Mr. Carlisle," he says. "You were in the room. You are a smart man. You had to know something was wrong. Why did you not walk away? Why did you not say something?"

I pause.

"I did not see it clearly at first. Later, I convinced myself I could limit the damage from inside. I stepped back from major cases. Walking away would not have changed the damage already done."

The session ends with formalities. They say they will be in touch.

I walk out. Greg waits in the hall.

I sit on a bench.

"They were not only asking about conduct," I say.

Greg studies me. Then he speaks.

"They were deciding if you are worth saving."

He checks his phone. His face tightens.

"Ben, we have a bigger problem," he says. "One of the panelists called me. They uncovered something buried. They say it's bad."

Chapter 18

Free Fall

In sports, the breaking point rarely comes in the final play. It comes earlier in a missed block, a misread defense, a sideline argument. The collapse starts in quiet moments, long before the scoreboard shows it. Law is no different. Firms don't fall all at once. They fracture, partner by partner, whisper by whisper, until what once held everyone together can't hold anyone at all.

A headline appears on my phone: **"Senior Hamilton Reed Partner Resigns Amid Ongoing DOJ Scrutiny."**

No name shows in the headline. I scan the article.

In the second paragraph, I see it: Elliot Gaines. He is one of the firm's top rainmakers. He has been with Hamilton Reed for over twenty years. He brought major corporations to the firm.

First Briggs. Now Gaines. Elliot is taking twenty partners with him. They are starting a Dallas office for Franklin & Sanders.

The firm lured him with more money if he brought enough partners.

Not long ago, I helped contain the Blackwood scandal. I kept it from trial.

If I were not under investigation, Elliot would have included me.

My phone vibrates. It's a text from Lucas Hayes, an associate I mentored.

"Heard about Gaines taking twenty partners. What's going on, Ben?"

Before I reply, another text arrives. This one is from Ken Stratton, a friend and client.

"Is Hamilton Reed collapsing? Should I be worried?"

Both texts reflect the same panic.

I call Ty McCrady in the Houston office. We tried a case together early on.

"It's bad," he says. "Renfro and Sadler left yesterday. No goodbyes. They took clients to Porter Hedges. Miller is interviewing there. His office is half-empty."

"Brooke is scrambling," he adds. "She makes promises she cannot keep."

Taylor Voss calls next. She is a junior partner who worked for me.

"Brooke came to my office this morning," she says. "She calls it a listening tour. She wants to stop younger partners from leaving."

"What is she doing?"

"She asks people to sign a loyalty letter."

"What does it say?"

"We support current leadership. We agree not to speak publicly without approval."

The day passes with calls and emails from colleagues and clients. Everyone asks the same questions.

Late afternoon, Ken Stratton asks to meet for coffee downtown.

We find a corner table in a crowded café.

“You stepped back from our matters,” he says. “How long will that last?”

“I turned over what I knew to the DOJ. I am cooperating. That is all I can say.”

He nods. “We may pull our files. I need a reason to stay.”

"I stepped back to protect Dallas lawyers who had nothing to do with Los Angeles. Once they crossed lines, I could not practice as if everything was normal."

"That is what I needed to hear," he says.

He stands. "We will move our files to another firm this week. I wish it were different."

He shakes my hand and leaves.

I sit alone at the table.

That afternoon, another article appears. It quotes Brooke Chandler: "We remain united and continue to serve clients with excellence."

I scroll past it.

Late that night, a legal blog posts an anonymous tip: Sources say the Dallas office is fracturing and may seek a merger partner.

My phone rings. Michael Levin.

"Did you see the blog post?"

"Yeah."

"The DOJ will move soon. That post was a warning. The State Bar will ask why you did not report sooner. Talk to your ethics lawyer."

The firm is not collapsing yet. But the cracks show.

Chapter 19
Bianca's Gambit

In sports, the biggest plays don't happen under the lights. They happen in film rooms, in sideline whispers, in moments no one sees. The win goes to the team that strikes first and hides its hand longest. Law isn't any different. It rewards preparation over power, timing over truth.

#

I'm barely awake when my phone buzzes. It's a message from Michael Levin:

Secure Zoom meeting in ten minutes.

I slip into the study and close the door. Erin sleeps down the hall.

I boot up the laptop and log on.

Michael appears. His sweatshirt is wrinkled. He has been up for hours.

"They went around us," he says.

"Who?"

"Bianca. She met with the DOJ last night. By herself."

"With counsel?"

"No. She called them directly. They logged it as an informal proffer."

"She gave a statement?"

"Enough to frame you."

"What did she say?"

"She claims you went rogue. You hired the investigator on your own. You ran communications outside the firm. You kept leadership in the dark."

"She said that?"

"She said you pressured her to hold off on the internal review. You insisted everything stay off the books."

"She's lying."

"Of course. But they are listening. You are the easier story. She is young, trying to rein things in."

"She is building her immunity play."

He nods. "She wants you to be the bad guy."

I should have seen it coming.

"What do we do?"

"You build your side. Now with timeline. Documents, and anything else that shows her direction."

"Has DOJ requested anything?"

"They want firm emails and memos. They pulled the trigger overnight. IT is imaging the archive."

"She is calculated."

"She saw this coming and moved first."

"You need to get ahead, quietly. No press. No confrontations. Just facts."

"I will start now."

"Do not assume she is done. This is her first move."

He signs off.

I open files. I sort emails and texts from Bianca.

I open my calendar for meetings and calls.

By sunrise, I sort everything into three folders: Neutral, Protective, and Dangerous.

I back up the folders and lock the drive in my safe.

New alert:

Dallas Partner May Have Engineered Cover-Up in Robinson Case

It appears on a legal blog.

I click. The language matches Bianca's. Truth mixed with lies.

It starts with the private investigator. It ends with a claim I kept LA leadership in the dark.

Comments flood in.

Clients suspend work. One wants a call to reassess matters.

A junior partner texts: "Bianca says you did this to impress Blackwood."

This goes beyond what DOJ does. It's my reputation.

Bianca leaked the story.

I call Michael.

"You saw it," he says.

"She is framing me."

"The leak has her fingerprints."

"Any legal moves?"

"Not without making it worse. Challenge her and it looks like retaliation."

"Then we wait?"

"For now. Build your record."

I call Rachel.

She answers.

"You saw the article?"

"I saw it. Bianca leaked it through her LA reporter."

"She says I went rogue."

"She is coaching associates to say she had no clue."

"Will you talk to DOJ?"

"I might. But not without a plan."

I thank her and end the call.

Cassidy Knox calls. I let it go to voicemail.

I call Kip Sutter.

"We might have to testify about the files showing Bianca orchestrated the takedown of Savannah."

"Okay, tell me when."

I spread out the documents under my desk lamp.

Emails from Bianca. Notes. Calendar entries.

One message: "Let me worry about the press. You keep the judge happy."

Another: "Do whatever it takes for Blackwood. We need results."

A text: "You have the spine, Ben. Do what you do."

I close the laptop.

Michael calls.

"They are deciding whether to charge you or list you as an unindicted co-conspirator. It depends on what Bianca gives next."

I look out the window.

The city stays quiet.

She bets I will not fight.

She is wrong.

Chapter 20
Countermeasures

In sports, there's a moment late in the game when you're no longer playing to win. You're playing not to lose. In football, it's protecting the ball and running down the clock. In basketball, it's spreading the floor and avoiding turnovers. In baseball, it's bringing in your closer and hoping no one gets on base. The strategy shifts. You protect the ball, limit risk, and stop chasing plays that aren't there.

Law is no different. When your law firm is under investigation, outnumbered, and already painted as the villain, you stop swinging for headlines. You protect your position., You protect the record. You control what you can and wait for your moment. Because one wrong move now doesn't just cost the case. It buries the law firm.

#

The morning after Bianca's version goes public, my phone does not stop.

Michael calls first.

"We have seen the leak impact. Clients are calling off meetings. Some are pulling work," he says.

"She moved first."

"She did. DOJ is watching the firm too."

"Are you ready?"

"I have to be."

"We need a full timeline. Every call, email, text that shows Bianca directed or knew."

I spend the day digging through the folders.

I find emails where Bianca insisted on "a tight ship."

I find a calendar invite: Meet Bianca. Urgent. Do not share.

I find texts from Bianca: "Handle it quietly, Ben."

Cassidy Knox calls.

"I heard the news," she says. "This is a mess."

"It is."

"If you want to fight, we need witnesses. People who saw the real Bianca."

"I am gathering everything."

"Good. Because this will get nasty."

Calls and texts continue from colleagues and clients.

A senior partner offers cautious support. Another says they are repositioning teams.

I block it out. I reconstruct the chain of decisions.

I think about Rachel. If she steps forward, it changes everything.

But she is scared.

I call Rachel again.

She answers on the third ring.

"I need to know if you will talk to DOJ," I say.

Pause.

"I have thought about it all day," she says. "Bianca called me this morning."

"What did she say?"

"She asked if I remembered things her way. She said the firm would protect me if I stayed quiet. She offered a transfer to San Francisco with a promotion to income partner and more money."

"And if you do not?"

"She did not say. But her voice changed."

Rachel exhales. "I kept the memos. The ones she approved."

"Will you give them to Michael?"

Another pause.

"Yes. But I need protection. Whistleblower status. Something."

"I will tell Michael. He will arrange it."

"Thank you, Ben."

She ends the call.

Rachel stepping forward changes the balance.

Bianca will know soon, and she will make another move.

I bundle the evidence and send it to Michael's secure drive.

Tomorrow, we meet with a forensic team to review the servers.

This time, I move first.

The fight has begun.

Chapter 21
Erin's Ultimatum

In basketball, when the shot clock winds down, you don't always get the play you drew up. Sometimes you're stuck in the corner, out of time and out of options. You force a shot and hope it lands. In law, and in life, those moments reveal what matters most.

#

Three days have passed since I told Erin about what I am facing.

Most of that time has been spent in the study, fielding calls and reviewing documents. Sleep comes in short stretches.

Erin checks in from time to time. She brings coffee and asks whether I have heard from Michael. Each time I thank her, tell her I am close, and promise I need a little more time.

Tonight I leave the study around nine. The house is quiet, the television off and her laptop closed.

I find her in the kitchen, standing at the counter with a water glass in her hand, her phone lying face down beside it.

She looks up when I walk in.

"We need to talk," she says.

I stop in the doorway. "Okay."

She does not sit. I stay standing.

"I cannot do this anymore," she says. "Not like this."

I lean against the kitchen island. "You mean the investigation?"

"I mean us. You barely talk. You don't sleep. When I ask, you say it is complicated.

"It is."

"Then make it less complicated. Or walk away. I cannot keep standing next to a man who is somewhere else."

"This is not permanent."

"That is what you said six months ago."

"You want me to quit?"

"No. I want you to decide if anything matters besides the firm or the case. If it does not, I need to know now."

"I did not ask for this."

"I know. But you did not stop it either. You kept saying you were handling it."

"I am."

"Then why do I find out about subpoenas from the news? Why did Cassidy ask me at lunch if you were okay?"

My phone buzzes in my pocket. The urgent vibration. From Locke or worse.

My hand moves to my pocket, then stops.

Erin watches.

The phone buzzes again.

"What did you tell her?"

"I said you are fine. Then I realized I do not know if that is true."

"I know you are not cheating. But you are not here. I am tired of asking you to come back."

She walks past me.

Her footsteps climb the stairs, leaving the kitchen quiet.

My phone shows two unread messages. None from Erin.

The briefcase comes with me into the study, where I sit at the desk and open the laptop. The screen still shows the timeline for a possible indictment. My name is not redacted. That's not reassuring.

After a moment, I close the computer.

Rachel's last email waits in my inbox, the scan she feared would disappear.

I leave it unopened. I already know what it says.

Preston Locke's name appears below. Flagged. Subject: *Need to talk.*

I mark it unread.

By midnight, I set our coffee machine to turn on at 6 a.m., and I head upstairs. Our bedroom door is closed. She wants to be alone, so I leave it closed.

In the guest room, I lie down fully clothed.

At dawn, I go downstairs and pour coffee into my travel mug before the house stirs.

A note from Erin is on the table by the door.

Client dropped off edits. I will be out most of the morning.

After folding the note and sliding it into my pocket, I pause at the door for a moment before stepping into the garage.

The engine starts and the street beyond the driveway is still empty.

A few minutes later, I turn into the mostly empty parking garage downtown, pull into my space, and walk toward the elevator bank.

My phone buzzes with messages. None are from Erin.

****

Bianca's Turn: Misdirection

Los Angeles. Same morning.

They will say I moved too fast. Let them.

I saw it coming before Ben hesitated. Before Chandler went quiet. Before Locke acted like he had principles.

Ben mistook silence for strength. I never have. He believed restraint would shield him. I know it doesn't.

I gave the DOJ enough to steer their attention, enough to fit the story they wanted.

Ben should have seen it coming. He handled the Robinson case well and made her look like exactly what the jury believed she was—a gold-digger chasing a payout.

I thought he could carry more than that. Then he pushed back on my terms. That was his mistake.

He believed he could win the case and walk away clean. Let the jury judge Robinson and let the rest of it disappear with the verdict.

But I made sure the paper trail pointed somewhere else.

To him.

That wasn't betrayal. It was survival.

He thought it was strategy when I handed him the NDA drafts and told him to make them airtight, no loose ends. What he never noticed was that I was the loose end.

Robinson was leverage in the case. Ben simply used the tools he was given.

If DOJ asks, I will give them enough to make them wonder whether he crossed the line alone. Harassment disguised as defense.

They will never see how I built it that way from the start.

Let him wonder if I betrayed him or saved him.

The longer he is unsure, the slower he reacts.

I do not need the last word.

I need the next move.

Chapter 22

The Grand Jury Reconvenes

In tennis, the second serve isn't for aces. It's for survival. The first serve is bold, powerful, meant to win the point outright. But when it misses, the second serve demands control, placement, nerves. It tests whether the player can hold steady under pressure, knowing that one mistake ends the game. Law is no different. The second time you're called, you don't swing for victory. You keep the ball in play. You survive the point.

#

The call from Michael comes a little after seven.

I stand in the kitchen. My coffee has gone cold. Erin has already left.

"They want you back," Michael says. "Tomorrow."

"In Los Angeles?"

"In the federal building. Same room."

I open my computer. "I will book a flight this afternoon at three from DFW."

I give him my arrival time. He will have a car waiting. Same hotel.

"I will pack a bag," I say. "See you this evening."

Pause.

"This time it is about Bianca."

"She already testified?"

"For two hours. She claimed she had nothing to hide. She said you signed off on strategy, investigator memos, Rachel Wolfe's role."

"That is not true."

"I know. But they do not."

"What do they want from me?"

"They want you to explain why you did not know what happened behind the scenes. They may want you to look careless. You were lead counsel for Blackwood and defended him in the trial."

"If they think I am responsible, that puts me in the crosshairs."

"Right now, they see you as liar or witness. You decide which."

"I will stick to last time."

"You may need to adjust. They have new billing logs and memos Rachel flagged."

"They know she came to me?"

"Not yet. But they will."

Outside the window the street is empty.

After ending the call, I go upstairs. The suit from the dry cleaner hangs in plastic in the closet. It goes into the garment bag with the rest of what I will need in Los Angeles.

The flight lands a little after five local time. Traffic from LAX moves slowly, and the drive to the hotel takes nearly half an hour.

Michael and I eat downstairs before separating for the night. After returning to my room, I spend several hours reviewing the documents and preparing for the testimony scheduled the next morning. Sleep finally comes sometime after midnight—around two in the morning my time.

The next morning, we pass through security at the federal building and enter the grand jury suite. The same officers stand at the desk.

Inside the room everything looks familiar. Chairs surround the table just as before. Danielle Vaughn and another Assistant United States Attorney sit across from the witness chair, the stenographer beside them. The seal of the United States hangs on the wall behind them.

Michael waits outside.

Danielle Vaughn opens the questioning.

"Mr. Carlisle, we want to revisit the Blackwood case you won in court."

Questions begin with timelines and my as Blackwood's trial lawyer.

Then:

"Did you approve or direct outside investigators in the Robinson case?"

"No."

"Were you aware of private surveillance?"

"Not during the litigation."

"Did you see reports from those investigators?"

"Yes."

"When did you first see them?"

"Shortly before the trial."

"Who showed them to you?"

"Rachel Wolfe."

"Did Ms. Wolfe express concerns about how the information had been obtained?"

"She believed some of it had been misused."

"Misused how?"

"She believed it was gathered to pressure the plaintiff and damage her credibility at trial."

"Did you share those concerns with firm leadership?"

"No. Not immediately."

"Why not?"

"I needed to understand what I was looking at and prepare for what became a high-profile trial."

Vaughn hands a folder to her colleague.

"Ms. Rivers claims you reviewed the investigator's reports before trial and advised her to proceed rather than seek a settlement."

"That is not true."

"She claims you were copied on emails discussing surveillance as tactic."

"I was not aware of those emails."

"Do you deny participating in planning background investigations into Savannah Robinson?"

"I do."

"Did you speak with Ms. Wolfe after the report?"

"Yes."

"Did you encourage her to stay silent?"

"No."

"Did you tell anyone else?"

"No."

"Why not?"

"I needed to know if it was approved strategy or something Bianca hid."

"Now?"

"Now I believe it was deliberate."

Silence.

Vaughn asks more about details, memos, and meetings.

I answer with facts and dates of events, and I keep my opinions to myself.

After forty-seven minutes, Vaughn says I am free to go.

In the hallway, Michael waits.

"They do not believe me," I say.

"They do not believe anyone. That's their job."

We ride the elevator down.

Before the car leaves for LAX, he says, "You did not lie."

"No. But I did not tell her everything."

He nods.

The driver pulls away.

My phone shows texts from Locke and Brooke. I do not open them.

I land after six and drive home to a quiet house.

At the kitchen table I spread out my notes and review the Blackwood time entries before opening Rachel's folder.

One line: Consulting services outside formal litigation. 2.3 hours. No initials. Coded expert review.

That is cleanup.

I fold the recording back into the envelope and leave the drawer open.

Rachel never mentioned it before. When I asked why, she said she didn't want to go to jail. Only then did it make sense. In California, recording someone without their knowledge is illegal.

After plugging the drive into my laptop, a single audio file appears on the screen.

Rachel's voice comes first, quiet, recorded in her office. Bianca is on speaker.

"Make sure Robinson understands what we have," Bianca says. "Use the investigator if needed. If she knows what comes out in front of a jury, this case disappears before trial. Keep it off the books."

Rachel answers carefully. "That crosses lines. Using private investigators to pull medical records and threaten exposure isn't discovery."

Bianca doesn't hesitate. "Lines win cases. Handle it."

The recording ends.

Rachel captured Bianca giving the order. She never told me about it, and now I understand why.

Lucky for Bianca, the recording will never surface at trial. In Texas it would have ended her career.

The drive goes back into the envelope before the envelope returns to the drawer.

****

Bianca's Turn: The Long Game

Los Angeles — Same evening

The sun has set. I keep the office lights on.

Staying late sends a message that I am still here, working and not afraid of my future.

I know Ben testified again. I know what they asked. I know how he answered.

The DOJ makes sure information finds its way back to me. Quietly.

Ben has not called. He's deciding if I betrayed him or protected him.

I'm fine with either. Survival doesn't allow sentiment, so his uncertainty works for me.

Ben believed his work defending Blackwood would speak for itself. That served him until now. When prosecutors ask questions, that mindset becomes weakness.

I gave them a clear version. It was organized and consistent.

His was cautious, not like the confident trial lawyer I first met. Instead, he looks defensive and still believes restraint protects him.

Silence builds credibility only when no one else speaks. I spoke because someone had to.

If he brings Rachel's documents, it could change direction. It might help him. It might hurt me. But it would force public confrontation.

I don't think he's ready. Not yet.

I don't need to make him villain. I need the story to move away from me. It already has.

In Dallas, he reviews time entries. He builds his version. I understand. I never believed work would shield me. I knew Ben would think of his future and his family. I don't blame him for that.

If DOJ follows up, I respond. Until then, I wait.

In the meantime, I have nothing left to clean up, only things to monitor.

Before I leave, I send one email. I make it short and to the point. It reminds them I cooperate and it keeps me in the right column.

I turn off the lights. I lock the door. I walk out.

The building is quiet. While Ben wonders what happens next, I know.

Chapter 23
The Breaking Point

In football, the most brutal plays don't come from contact. They come from hesitation. One moment of indecision, and you miss the block, mistime the throw, leave the gap wide open. Law is no different. In a fractured firm, the worst damage comes not from those who act, but from those who wait too long to choose a side.

#

An email arrives at six a.m.

Meeting invite: Partners Only. Eight a.m. Main Dallas conference room.

I have not been to the office in weeks.

I arrive. The hallway outside the conference room stays quiet. No chatter.

I step inside. Lights are low. Half the chairs are filled.

Preston Locke sits at one end. Brooke sits across from him. Her posture stays relaxed.

McAllister's chair is empty.

No bagels. No coffee. Pitchers of water and glasses line the counter.

I take a seat. No one looks over.

Brooke clears her throat.

"We have been given an opportunity. We need to act fast."

She pauses.

"A major Houston firm wants to expand in Dallas. They will bring us in as a full office. New leadership. Infrastructure support."

She names Callahan & Yates.

Brooke would lead the transition.

She frames it as survival, pointing to client losses, DOJ visibility, and reputational risk.

Her eyes settle on me briefly.

"Some names carry more weight than others now. Not in a good way."

She does not say my name.

A few partners glance my way, then look down.

Locke speaks.

"Dissolving the firm is surrender. We lost direction when we chased growth. But we can fix that."

He looks at Brooke.

"This office still has a core."

Older partners nod. Younger ones shift.

Brooke does not back off.

"You're right, Preston. But we will not keep any of it if we are sued out of existence."

She names three lawsuits tied to Blackwood.

"Even Dallas is exposed. If they hit before we control the narrative, we defend conduct and culture. If we act quickly, we contain the damage."

Murmurs ripple around the table.

"Leadership requires clarity," Brooke says. "Uncertainty invites collapse."

Partners look at me.

I lean forward.

"This is about who we want to be. Do we remain Hamilton Reed or fold into Callahan & Yates?"

I pause before continuing.

"Callahan & Yates wants us now. Once they have us, we become second-class."

No one interrupts.

"I made mistakes. I stayed quiet too long. But calling this a merger is not leadership. It's a retreat."

I look around the table.

"If we break apart now, we're not protecting our clients. We're protecting ourselves."

The room stays quiet.

"If reputation is the issue, we rebuild it. If liability is the issue, we face it together."

Brooke gathers her papers.

"We will call for a vote."

She walks out. A few partners follow. A younger partner stands, gathers his pad, and walks out without a word, following Brooke.

Locke stays.

Cassidy Knox stays.

Tom Whitfield says, “We rebuild. Smaller firm. People who believe in what this firm once was.”

I nod. “We start with the Los Angeles claims. I will take the lead resolving them.”

Someone across the table says, “Without money, we will not survive.”

Locke answers before anyone else can respond. “We do not need to grow fast. We need to grow right. Our Texas clients still want that.”

No one cheers, but it is a start.

Locke and I leave the room together and step into a hallway that is already half empty. Files are stacked along the walls, and several nameplates are gone.

We pass Brooke’s office. The door is closed, and neither of us slows down.

Chapter 24

The Next Play

In football, when the original game plan falls apart, you stop running the plays you practiced all week. Your quarterback is rattled. Your star receiver is doubled. The defense knows your tendencies. So you adapt. You go back to basics. You trust the players who are still in the huddle and find a way to move the ball forward.

Law firms work the same way. When your firm is breaking apart, you stop clinging to the old structure and start asking who is still standing beside you. The question isn't whether the firm has changed. The question is whether you still want to play, and who you want on your team.

#

Late the next evening a message arrives from Preston.

My office. 7:30. Just you.

I arrive ten minutes early and park in the garage beneath the building before riding the elevator up alone. The reception floor is dark except for motion lights along the hallway.

When I reach Preston's office a few minutes later, his door is slightly open. I step inside.

He sits behind his desk with his jacket off and his sleeves rolled up, a coffee cup half full beside him.

"Close the door," he says.

After I do, he gestures toward the chair across from him.

"We are starting over," he says. "Without Brooke. She is taking a group to Callahan & Yates."

I nod.

"I want your help."

Preston walks to the window and stands there with his hands in his pockets while the morning light cuts through the glass.

"We are starting over," he says. "Without Brooke. She is taking a group to Callahan & Yates."

"Hamilton Reed will not survive the next month," he says. "The DOJ is not finished. Lawsuits are coming from Los Angeles. At least five women. All tied to Blackwood. Surveillance. Smear campaigns. Threats."

"Class action?"

“Maybe. They allege abuse of process and emotional distress. They target the firm for looking the other way.”

A slow breath escapes before the phone vibrates on the table.

Michael Levin.

Preston watches as I step into the hallway and answer.

“DOJ sent a forensic extract tied to the Blackwood billing servers.” Michael says.

For a moment my eyes close.

“It’s what I warned you about,” he continues. “Post–litigation-hold activity. Files weren’t lost. They were overwritten.”

“By who?”

A pause.

“Admin credentials tied to Los Angeles.”

“Mine?”

“No.”

Silence.

“They say it’s bad,” he adds.

I hang up and stand there trying to process what I just heard before going back into Preston’s office.

When I open the door, Preston is still at the window.

"We can't save this," I say.

Preston turns. "That bad?"

I nod. "Bad enough."

"I fought to keep it together. But too many lawyers are leaving. We won't survive what's coming."

He places a folder on the desk.

"I am building something new. Smaller. Texas offices only. No legacy name."

"Cassidy Knox and at least a dozen other Dallas partners are in. Branson and Dawson from Houston."

I pick up the folder.

Draft charter. List of names. Business plan.

Projected revenue. Office locations. Partner draws.

I close it.

"Who else knows?"

"The ones I asked. No announcements."

"If I say no?"

"We are short one litigator. But I will understand."

"If I say yes, I become the face while the Bar and press see me as the problem."

"Some will. But the ones who matter will not."

He waits.

"What do you want from me?"

"You lead litigation. You help create the culture we had before Los Angeles."

The room stays quiet.

The city wakes outside the windows.

Clients still call some of us directly. They ask about stability. They ask if we are staying.

Preston knows that.

"If we wait too long, the window closes. Press, Bar, plaintiffs will decide the story."

He sits again.

"This is not about loyalty to me. It is about whether the work is still worth doing."

I stay quiet.

I think about the last partners' meeting. Brooke walked out with her group. Locke stayed.

I think about the empty offices I passed this morning. Nameplates gone. Boxes stacked.

I think about Erin. She has not asked if I am joining Preston. She waits for me to decide.

I think about the recording in Rachel's envelope. If I join, I bring that fight with me.

Preston watches.

I open the folder again.

The list of names is short. Ten partners. Five associates.

No Brooke. No McAllister.

I close it.

"I need to see the numbers," I say.

He slides another page across.

Projected first-year revenue. Client commitments already in writing.

Some names I recognize. Clients who called me directly.

They want continuity, and they are calling me.

I look at Preston.

"When do we start?"

He nods once. "Next week. New leases signed yesterday. Smaller space downtown."

I stand. "I am in."

He stands too and extends his hand. I shake it. There is no celebration. Just the next play.

I walk out into a quiet hallway. Boxes line the walls. I pass my office. The files are still locked. Tessa's desk is empty.

I stop at the window overlooking the city. Traffic moves below.

The firm I joined is ending. Something new begins.

I do not know if it will work. But I am ready to find out.

Chapter 25
The Indictment List

In baseball, when the umpire's call doesn't go your way, you don't argue if you want to stay in the game. You keep your head down, take your stance, and wait for the next pitch. Even when the strike zone feels rigged, even when you know the last one was outside. Because getting thrown out means you're done, and staying in gives you one more swing.

Law is no different. The rulings aren't always fair. But once the government makes its move, lawyers don't argue with the DOJ. They regroup and figure out their next move because the case will still be tried. And what comes next matters most.

#

I come back to the office the next morning knowing this might be the day.

The DOJ issues the press release at 10:02 a.m. The link hits my inbox less than a minute later. I click it open.

The headline reads:

Department of Justice Announces Federal Indictments in Hamilton Reed Case.

I scan the first paragraph. Three names. Bianca Rivers. Evan Marston. Blake Emory. Three California partners who thought they were untouchable.

My name is not there.

I knew it would not be. But seeing it official makes it real.

Texts arrive. Headlines. Calls I do not answer.

The third paragraph lists unindicted co-conspirators. They do not use names. They use numbers.

Unindicted Co-Conspirator #3.

The timeline matches mine. The role matches. Anyone paying attention will connect it soon. Reporters will read between the lines. Clients will too.

The charges follow. Obstruction. Witness tampering. Conspiracy. Racketeering. A pattern of covert settlements, punctuated by the occasional courtroom victory. Intimidation. Surveillance used to silence victims. Misrepresentations to the SEC. Destruction of electronically stored information after a litigation hold.

I stop reading.

I am not indicted. But I am not cleared.

The DOJ left me out for a reason. They expect testimony. If I hold back, they add my name later.

My phone buzzes again. Michael from Los Angeles.

“You seeing this?”

“I am.”

“You are not on it.”

“I know. But I am in it.”

“They kept you in play. Your testimony gets convictions. If you slip, they charge you.”

I lean back. The office stays quiet. Most lawyers have not come in. Boxes line the hallways.

I call Preston Locke.

“You saw it?” he asks.

“I did.”

“You are not on it.”

“But I am in it.”

There is a pause.

"Let's keep going," he says.

We hang up.

I sit at my desk with nothing to do. Clients still call some days. They ask about stability. They ask if I am staying.

I think about the new firm Preston described. Smaller. Texas only.

I think about Erin. She has not asked if I am joining. She waits.

My phone rings again. Bianca.

I stare at the name and let it go to voicemail. She does not leave a message.

I open the press release again and read the charges slowly. Surveillance on Savannah Robinson. Threats through investigators. NDAs used to silence. Billing coded to hide expenses.

I close the window.

Rachel's envelope sits in my drawer. The thumb drive inside. Her recording of Bianca directing intimidation.

If I hand it over, it ends Bianca. But it risks Rachel. It risks me if the DOJ sees it as late.

I leave the drawer closed. For now.

The phone buzzes again. A text from Rachel.

Saw the indictment. You okay?

I type "Yes," and then I delete it. I type "We need to talk" and send it. She replies: *Tonight?*

I type *Yes* and set the phone down.

The indictment changes everything. And nothing.

Bianca walks free for now. But the trial comes.

I will be the star government witness.

The question is what I say when I am.

Chapter 26

Fallout

In boxing, it's not always the knockout that ends the fight. Sometimes the real loss comes in the next round, when the fighter stands up, dazed and bleeding, and has to keep swinging. Law is no different. The punch lands. The headline hits. But the damage shows later, when the calls stop coming and the silence settles in.

The phone keeps ringing. I stare at the screen. It's Bianca. Finally, I answer.

"Ben," she says. Her voice stays smooth.

I do not speak.

"I thought you would want to hear it from me," she says. "I saw the press release. We both knew this day was coming. But it's not over."

I wait.

"They will come after me," she says. "They will use you to do it. But you and I know the truth is more complicated."

I stay quiet.

"You need to clear this up now," she says. "Tell them what really happened. What you saw. What you did not."

I don't respond.

"You were part of this firm. We built something. They are burning it down. You think they will stop with me?"

She pauses.

"You were always careful, Ben. That is what I liked about you."

She says it like a compliment. It isn't.

Before I respond, she ends the call.

I set the phone down and don't pick it back up. I understand her. She's trying to stay in control.

The firm name is finished. Clients don't want to retain us. Recruits don't want to put the firm name on their résumés.

Cassidy Knox tell me that our Houston office says that four of their clients will stick us. They want clarity from us. Preston drafts an outline, and I trim promises that we cannot keep.

"You think that makes us look uncertain?" he asks.

I understand his concern, but I disagree. "I think it makes us look honest," I say.

He sends it. Read receipts appear, meaning it's been received. But no one replies that day.

I hang up.

The fallout is not over. It keeps spreading.

Preston and I spend the next three days making calls to old clients and longtime contacts. Those who used to return messages within the hour now take days, or don't respond at all. One of my top clients answers on the first ring and cuts straight to it.

"We like you, Ben. But we can't bring this to our board. Not while you're still mentioned in the DOJ filings."

I thank him for letting me know.

Some of my clients listen. A few of them agree to meet. They make no commitments, but at least they don't hang up. That counts for something.

We set up meetings in offices we no longer control, borrow boardrooms from friends, and keep the lights on with a patchwork of favors and whatever retainer money hasn't been clawed back. We don't have a firm yet. We have a list of names, a few files, and the belief that starting over still beats walking away. We have maybe three weeks before the money runs out. After that, we're negotiating from zero.

Later that afternoon, I walk down the hall past empty offices. One assistant is boxing up framed certificates that had been on the wall of the lawyer she assisted. Another lady peels a nameplate off the wall by a former partner's door.

Cassidy calls again.

"You see the email from Branson?" she asks.

"Not yet."

"Houston's floating new names and they want the name by Monday."

"We may not meet that deadline," I say.

I hear a sigh, and before I can offer anything else, she hangs up.

The next morning, we meet with a longtime client at their office in The Crescent Center. Preston wears a conservative navy suit and lets me take the lead. I once won a patent infringement case for them. Helen, their general counsel, is sharp, direct, and doesn't waste time.

"Let me be clear," she says as soon as we sit down. "I took this meeting because I respect the work you've done for us. But our board is nervous. They want assurances."

"You're not getting a press release," I say. "We came to see you in person. We'll tell you what we know, what we don't, and what we can still do."

Helen studies me, then looks to Preston.

"Who else is staying with you?"

"Cassidy Knox. Taylor Voss. Branson and Dawson from Houston," Preston says.

"And you, Ben?" she asks. "They haven't indicted you, but they haven't given you complete immunity either. What happens if the DOJ isn't satisfied with your testimony and your name ends up on the next press release?"

I nod slowly. "I understand your concern. I can't control what the DOJ does. But I've told the truth, and I'll keep doing that. You've seen my work. You know how I handle what's in front of me. That hasn't changed."

Helen doesn't smile, but she leans back in her chair. "I appreciate your honesty. I can't promise anything. But I'll bring this back to the board."

We stand. She offers her hand.

"Good luck. You're going to need it," she says.

"Luck doesn't build a firm," I say. "Clients do. And we're not done yet."

She leaves it at that.

Later that night, I rewrite a letter to a client I haven't heard from since before the indictments. I keep it simple with no marketing language or spin. I write what I know, what I don't, and what I'm willing to stand behind now. I delete the first two drafts and send the third.

I don't hear back that night or the next morning. Then, shortly after noon, a reply comes in.

"Let's talk. Monday. 10 AM."

I read it twice, close the laptop, and lean back in my chair. My home office is quiet. Erin is in the family room watching television.

I open the file for Monday's meeting, trim language that sounds like an explanation, and remove two lines that are only partially true. Then I save it and close the file.

By Friday, the tone shifts. It's not on paper, or in court. But it's there.

Calls that used to end quickly now linger. Preston hears from a friend at DOJ that my name is no longer on the internal summaries labeled *subjects under review*. Another lawyer says I've been moved to the *witness stack*, the internal list of people they expect to testify but don't plan to charge. No one explains it officially. I've done this long enough to recognize when a line has been redrawn, and I may have crossed to the other side of it.

I don't say anything to Erin. I don't say anything to Preston.

Michael Levin calls Saturday morning.

"They want your testimony," he says. "Not as a target. As a witness."

I don't say a word.

"I've spoken with Vaughn's team. They're not offering you immunity or a deal, but they're not naming you in the next round of filings."

I don't relax. But I sit up straighter.

"They'll fly you out next week. You'll meet with Vaughn's people, go through your notes, and answer questions. That's it."

"Understood."

"One more thing," Michael says. "I don't need to remind you of this, but I will anyway. Don't guess. Don't embellish. Stick to what you saw, what you knew at the time, what you signed. You want to helpful yourself? Be accurate, and as important, be boring."

I fly out Monday afternoon. I didn't get the upgrade, so I'm stuck in coach. The seat is cramped. The cabin is quiet. I skip the drink and close my eyes, but sleep doesn't come. I land at LAX just before sunset, take a cab in heavy rush hour traffic downtown, and check into a hotel across from the courthouse. The room has floor to ceiling windows with a view of downtown. The bed is plush, but it doesn't matter, I don't sleep well.

Michael meets me in the lobby the next morning. He's dressed in the same pin-stripe tailored suit he wore last time. We cross the street to the US Courthouse. After going through security, we take the elevator to the second floor and find the office. Inside, Vaughn's team is waiting. There are two prosecutors and a paralegal with a thick stack of files. A court reporter is already setting up.

They don't waste time.

Danielle Vaughn asks the questions. The younger lawyer watches. She goes back to when I saw edits to the Savannah Robinson press release, when I flagged the issue to Bianca, what she said, and what she didn't.

She asks about meetings, documents, decisions, silence. I answer the same way I always have. I stick to what I saw, what I signed, and what I knew.

Once, when the questions edge toward speculation, I cut in first.

"I don't know what she was thinking. I only know what she said to me."

Vaughn seems satisfied.

After two hours, she closes the file and thanks me. Michael and I walk out the same way we came in.

Outside, the sky is gray. Barricades sit stacked near the courthouse steps. Press trucks are parked nearby. It's quiet now, but it won't be by the end of the week.

"They'll want you in the witness room when the trial starts Monday," Michael says.

"Got it."

He looks at me a moment longer. "You ready?"

"I've been ready since the day she made that call."

He nods and walks away.

I head back to the hotel and sit at the desk. There's nothing to prepare. I already know what I'll say.

That night, I eat dinner at the bar downstairs. A young woman sits beside me. She's not the first to have sat next to me at a bar in Los Angeles. By now, I understand, that it's not just for small talk. I tap my ring finger. She notices and moves on.

Chapter 27
Opening Moves

#

In any high-stakes game, the first quarter isn't about winning. It's about setting the tone.

Coaches script the opening series not just to score but to test the defense, control tempo, and show who's in charge. The smart ones know: momentum doesn't wait. You take it, or you chase it the rest of the way.

Trials start the same way. The government's opening statement isn't always meant to convince. It's meant to corner. To shape what the jury sees before the defense ever speaks.

#

Bianca's Turn:

Los Angeles. Monday morning.

The federal courthouse rises in hard angles, steel and concrete built to intimidate. It was not designed to welcome. It was designed to judge those who enter, including me.

Outside, the sidewalk is crowded with cameras, microphones, and cardboard signs. I hear the chants before I step from the car.

"Justice for Savannah!"

"Hold the lawyer accountable."

"Blackwood destroyed her in court,"

They chant her name. That is the story Vaughn wants the jury to believe. She does not need evidence if she has outrage first.

Most of the crowd is not organized. They are angry. That has been the pattern since the Me Too movement took hold. Some hold screenshots pulled from blogs and social media. Others shove phones in my face, live-streaming as I walk past.

The security detail keeps the line moving. Former state officials, professional and disciplined. They do not draw weapons. They do not touch anyone. They form a presence that discourages confrontation without inviting spectacle.

I walk up the steps without breaking stride, eyes forward, no reaction. They want a villain. They want a moment they can replay all afternoon. I did not rise from middle-class obscurity to the top of a Los Angeles law firm by losing control in public. Perception is not fixed. It is a longer game. Let them fill the silence however they want. I am not giving them the story they came for.

Inside, metal detectors and X-ray machines create a bottleneck. Marshals recognize me. One checks my ID. Another waves me through. It is not friendliness. It is routine. Federal court does not care who you are until you are on the record.

David Kellogg waits outside Courtroom 9B. He does not smile.

"Our judge is Simone Dubois," he says. "Recently assigned. You know her."

I do. I've tried cases in her courtroom. Appointed by President Obama, she has a reputation for thoughtfulness and a quiet liberal streak, but no one calls her soft. She is tough on white-collar defendants. She respects preparation. She respects discipline. She will not make this easy.

My lawyer, David Kellogg opens the door. I enter first, and he follows.

The courtroom is half full. Press in the gallery. Clerks setting water and microphones. The government team occupies the left table. Danielle Vaughn sits with her laptop open, yellow legal pad squared beside it. Her posture tells the jury she is ready for their verdict.

I take my seat at the defense table.

Evan Marston stares straight ahead. Blake Emory leans toward his lawyer. They hired me. Mentored me. Ran the office. Now we face prison together.

Jury selection becomes a war of attrition. Kellogg uses strikes carefully. Vaughn plays the long game. A few jurors slip through. An older woman in the second row watches steadily. A young man in the back glances at me more than once.

I don’t need all twelve. I need one.

Judge Dubois enters, robe settling as she takes the bench. The jurors file in.

Vaugn opens. She walks them through secret settlements, surveillance of accusers, and legal threats designed to intimidate. She mentions the Robinson trial as the rare case that reached a jury before describing the pattern that followed. Then she names Ben Carlisle as the reluctant witness who defended Blackwood in the Robinson trial and later finally realized what was happening. He spoke up. We tried to silence him.

Then she sharpens her focus on me. I orchestrated it. Evan and Blake participated. And when scrutiny finally came, evidence did not disappear by accident.

The story is clean. It is dangerous. It is wrong.

Kellogg rises.

He buttons his jacket and walks to the podium without notes. He begins with a story about a street game called three-card monte on Venice Beach. The game is not about the cards. It is about where you are looking.

He draws the parallel with precision. The prosecution wants headlines, outrage, and emails stripped of context. They want the jury focused on Bianca Rivers, not on the firm's history or what existed long before I arrived.

Aggressive lawyering is not a crime. There were no illegal payments. No intent to obstruct justice. Trials are not won on emotion. They are won on evidence. We are not here to prove innocence. The government must prove guilt.

A few jurors nod. One scribbles notes.

Evan's lawyer stands next. He distances Evan from me. Limited knowledge. Delegated authority.

Blake's lawyer follows. He creates more distance. The mistakes were mine.

I keep my expression neutral.

We sat in the same meetings, developed the same trial strategies, and signed the same NDAs.

Now we are no longer partners. Now I hold the bag.

Chapter 28
Counterpunching

#

In boxing, it's not the hardest punch that wins. It's the one that lands when your opponent doesn't see it coming.

In law, trials aren't built on facts. They're built on impressions.

#

Bianca's Turn: Taking the Punches

Los Angeles – The government's case unfolds

Contrary to what the general public might think, trials are not about truth. They are more about perception. You can see it every day on Court TV.

Danielle Vaughn has a reputation for winning white-collar cases in Los Angeles. She looks and acts confident. I hired David Kellogg because he is one of the very few LA lawyers who wins federal white collar criminal cases.

I sit at the defense table, shoulders straight, hands visible. Posture matters. Jurors notice how you carry yourself, especially when your name is not spoken.

Over the next two days, I expect Vaughn to build their version of the story. Witness by witness, they will likely sketch me as the one who knew the surveillance was off the books, approved the billing codes that hid it, and pushed the Robinson case forward anyway.

Vaughn starts with Kyra Sands, FBI forensic analyst. Sands looks you and polished, but comes across as over-prepared.

Sands walks the jury through metadata and communications. Exhibit numbers. Timestamps. Screenshots.

She connects billing codes to SEC drafts, calendar invites, and memo changes Ben flagged. She makes it sound surgical. Damning.

She explains edits from my account. Internal warnings ignored. She draws no conclusions. She lets the jury do the math.

I do not look at the screen. Let them stare. Let them wonder why I stay calm.

The truth is that edits were made, some by me and some by others. The timing fits their narrative, not mine.

Jurors believe what sounds clear and decisive, not explanations that ask them to weigh subtleties.

David Kellogg stands and buttons his jacket. He looks at the jury, and then waits half a beat.

His voice is warm, grandfatherly, but his questions cut.

"Miss Sands, have you run a business?"

"No."

He nods as if the point is obvious.

"Have you made high-stakes decisions under a deadline, with legal, financial, and client pressure?"

"No."

He nods. "Yet you understand intent behind edits?"

"I explain technical links."

"No, you interpret them. You turn footprints into motive."

Vaughn objects. "Argumentative."

"Overruled."

Kellogg repeats. "You claim to understand intent?"

"No."

"Exactly. That's the jury's job."

He gestures to the jury gently.

Vaughn objects again. Judge Dubois sustains and instructs Kellogg not to characterize.

Kellogg undercuts calmly. He reminds them inference is not proof. He walks Sands into admitting some logs could include delegated edits.

His tone is polite. But he shows contrast. Sands sound careful and rehearsed. Kellog has made that clear to the jury.

Kellogg returns to the table.

Evan's lawyer stands. He distances Evan.

"Miss Sands, do you see Mr. Marston's name on these emails?"

"No."

"Is there any indication he authorized anything that you found?"

"No."

Blake's lawyer is sharper.

"Was Mr. Emory in the chain?"

"Yes, copied."

"But no responses or edits by him?"

"No."

Vaughn does not waste a redirect with Sands. She focuses on the metadata that traces the billing approvals to my account. The emails show when the investigator's reports arrived, when the billing codes were entered, and when the Robinson case moved forward.

According to the government, the timing proves I directed was happening.

I sit still. I know what they are doing.

They take the spaces between those events and fill them with intent.

Judge Dubois adjusts her glasses and turns to Vaughn. "Call your next witness."

Vaughn rises. She does not look at me.

"The government calls Special Agent Mark Ellison."

A man in a dark suit takes the stand. He looks like he's in his late forties and calmly takes his seat in the witness chair with FBI posture, but without the stiffness. Ellison's not here to persuade. He is here to explain.

He swears in.

Vaughn walks him through credentials quickly. Digital forensics. Computer intrusion. Evidence recovery. Years of it. The jury listens without excitement. This is not a human story. Not yet.

"Agent Ellison," Vaughn says, "were you asked to examine electronic data from Hamilton Reed's Los Angeles office?"

"Yes."

"For what purpose?"

"To determine whether records relevant to the investigation had been altered or destroyed."

She pauses, letting the silence stretch.

"What did you find?"

Ellison does not raise his voice.

"After a litigation hold was issued, multiple files were overwritten on the firm's Los Angeles document management system."

He pauses long enough for the word to register. The files were not lost or misplaced. They were overwritten.

From the jury box I can see several jurors exchange looks. They understand exactly what that word means.

Vaughn presses a remote, and a simple timeline appears on the screen showing dates, file paths, and system logs.

"Can you explain what overwriting means in this context?" she asks.

Ellison answers in plain terms.

"It means new data was written over existing data in a way that prevents recovery."

"Accidental?"

"No."

"Routine system process?"

"No."

"Did it occur before or after the litigation hold?"

"After."

She does not ask who. Not yet.

"Was this activity traceable?"

"Yes."

"To what?"

"Administrative credentials assigned to the Los Angeles office."

She stops there, the way she always does. She avoids names and focuses only on the damage.

Kellogg pushes back his chair and stands. He buttons his jacket before stepping to the podium and takes his time before speaking.

"Agent Ellison," he says, "you cannot tell this jury who physically deleted or overwrote those files. Correct?"

"That's correct."

"You cannot tell them who was sitting at a keyboard."

"No."

"You cannot tell them whether the person who used those credentials was authorized to do so."

"Only that the credentials had administrative access."

"Shared access."

"Yes."

Kellogg nods, satisfied.

"And just to be clear," he adds gently, "you have no evidence my client, Bianca Rivers, personally deleted anything."

"No."

Evan's lawyer stands next. Shorter. Sharper.

"Agent Ellison, did you find any data showing Evan Marston initiated or approved deletion of files?"

"No."

"Any communication tying him to it?"

"No."

Blake's lawyer does not stand immediately. He waits.

"Agent Ellison," he says finally, "administrative credentials can be used by IT staff, outside vendors, or multiple partners. Correct?"

"Yes."

"So what you're telling this jury is something happened."

"Yes."

"But you cannot say who did it."

"That's correct."

Vaughn does not redirect.

She doesn't need to.

Ellison steps down.

I keep my hands flat on the table. Jurors look at me now, not because they know I did it, but because they're not sure I did anything wrong. Uncertainty is not innocence. But it is leverage.

Judge Dubois turns back to Vaughn.

"Call your next witness."

Vaughn rises. "The government Rachel Wolfe."

Rachel walks in. No makeup. Hair pulled back. Black blazer too big.

She swears to tell the truth.

Vaughn opens gently. "State your name and occupation."

"Rachel Wolfe. Attorney. Former associate at Hamilton Reed, Los Angeles."

Vaughn establishes timeline. Rachel joined Blackwood team early. She assisted me and Ben Carlisle. She reviewed drafts, coordinated edits, and submissions to regulators.

Then Vaughn has Rachel testify she submitted revised statements to SEC after I approved. I made the material changes.

Vaughn displays version history.

"This change in paragraph three. Do you recognize it?"

"Yes. Added by Ms. Rivers."

"Was it in your draft?"

"No."

"Did Ms. Rivers explain?"

"She said simplify. That's all."

Vaughn nods. "Did you believe it altered meaning?"

"Yes."

"In what way?"

"It downplayed risk."

Vaughn turns to internal email Rachel sent weeks later.

"I was concerned. Language was not consistent with internal facts."

"Did you raise with Ms. Rivers?"

"I tried."

"What happened?"

"She said it was filed and that changing anything now would create issues."

Rachel does not look at me. She cannot afford to. If she does, she will have to decide who betrayed whom first.

Vaughn returns to counsel table. "No further questions."

Kellogg stands and walks to the podium without notes.

"Ms. Wolfe, you were a fifth-year associate working on the Blackwood matter, correct?"

"Yes."

"You were familiar with the SEC filing process for that client?"

"Yes."

"That process required multiple drafts and internal review before anything was submitted to the SEC?"

"Yes."

"And nothing was submitted without approval from the partner supervising the matter?"

"Yes."

"You testified that Ms. Rivers made edits to the draft filings. Who submitted the final version?"

"I did, after she signed off."

"Did Ben Carlisle raise any concerns?"

"No."

Kellogg nods. "You had concerns about changes?"

"Yes."

"But you did not raise your concerns before you submitted the final version?"

"No."

"Did anyone stop you?"

"No."

"Did Ms. Rivers tell you to stay quiet?"

"No."

He pauses. "You came forward after the SEC inquiry?"

"Yes."

"And now you are here because the filing was misleading and you did not stop it."

"Yes."

Kellogg nods once.

"Ms. Wolfe, you testified Ms. Rivers approved the filing. That approval came after multiple partners reviewed the language, correct?"

Rachel hesitates. "Yes."

"Including Mr. Carlisle?"

"Yes."

Kellogg lets that sit. "No further questions."

He returns to the table.

Evan and Blake's lawyers just get Rachel to admit neither of them signed off on anything or directed Rachel to change anything.

Vaughn cleans up.

"Ms. Wolfe, you were junior associate reporting to senior partners?"

"Yes."

"You followed directions from Ms. Rivers and others?"

"Yes."

"You testified about your role, your discomfort, and your decision to come forward. Is there anything you are hiding?"

"No."

Vaughn sits.

I glance at the young juror in the back row. His arms are crossed. He is not convinced I'm a criminal.

I need him to stay that way. Because if he turns, the rest will follow.

Judge Dubois adjourns for the day.

We reconvene tomorrow.

Chapter 29
Shifting the Score

In sports, especially in the late innings or final quarters, momentum doesn't announce itself. It changes subtly. It might be a missed free throw, a dropped pass, or a hesitation on the base path. You don't always know the score is shifting until it's too late to adjust.

Likewise in law, trials don't tip on the big moment. They shift when no one's looking. Veteran court analysts see changes in phrasing, in posture, and in the weight a witness puts on one word instead of another. The lawyers call it nuance. Jurors call it doubt.

Bianca's Turn: Shifting the Score

Los Angeles – Tuesday Morning

The chants start again before the car even turns onto Spring Street. Different voices from yesterday, but carrying the same signs, as if someone paid to have them made. I suspect those carrying the signs are also being paid.

It may be an act, but when the TV cameras are on them, they are angry. Their chants claim I'm guilty and deserve punishment.

I stare ahead through the tinted glass. My security detail waits to open the door, but I don't move until the timing is right. Let the photographers jostle. Let the live streamers try to capture something raw. I've done this walk before. They want the woman from the headlines.

I straighten my shoulders and keep walking.

I walk up the courthouse steps, through the metal detectors, and past the voices that still echo behind the glass. The same marshals wave me through without making eye contact. It is routine.

Kellogg meets me outside the courtroom. His eyes sweep the gallery through the glass before he opens the door.

We step inside.

More heads turn this morning. Reporters lean forward over their notebooks, and several people in the gallery watch me take my seat at the defense table.

Kellogg settles beside me without speaking.

At the other table, my former partners sit with their lawyers again.

Judge Dubois enters from the side door. Everyone stands until she says, "You may be seated."

When the jurors are seated, she looks toward the government table.

"You may call your next witness."

Vaughn stands. "The government calls Eric Landon."

The door opens. Landon walks in wearing a dark suit and rimless glasses. He looks like every financial expert I've ever cross-examined, a numbers guy. I can tell he's an experienced witness.

All three defense lawyers rise together and agree without objection. He's an expert.

It takes the formality out of it and keeps the trial moving.

Vaughn starts slowly, letting him get comfortable. She walks him through his credentials. He's an Ivy League graduate with two decades in forensic accounting. He's been retained by both government agencies and private clients, testifying in over thirty trials.

Vaughn pivots to the disclosures.

"Mr. Landon, were you asked to analyze the SEC filings submitted on behalf of Blackwood Holdings during the regulatory inquiry?"

"Yes."

"And what were your findings?"

He doesn't hesitate. "There were omissions. Specifically, language that downplayed known risks related to litigation settlements and ongoing exposure was missing."

"Were those omissions material?"

"Yes."

He says it like it's obvious.

Vaughn clicks to display Exhibit 72. It's a chart comparing the original draft Rachel Wolfe prepared with the final version submitted to the SEC.

Landon narrates the changes. One section references a "resolved personnel matter." The earlier draft described it as a "Allegations of sexual harassment involving a high-profile executive." Landon calls that distinction significant. So does Vaughn.

She lets him explain how the omissions, even if not technically false, were misleading to investors, especially since what was left out involved the company's founder and CEO. He uses phrases like "duty of candor" and "reasonable investor standard."

Vaughn wraps the direct with one final question.

"In your expert opinion, Mr. Landon, would these omissions, if known, have altered the SEC's perception of the company's risk profile?"

"Yes."

"And would they have influenced investor decision-making?"

"In my opinion, absolutely."

She thanks him and sits.

Judge Dubois glances our way. "Mr. Kellogg, you may cross-examine."

"Thank you, Your Honor," Kellogg says while rising slowly.

He has no notes. A lawyer with his talent and memory doesn't need notes.

"Mr. Landon," he begins, "you've testified in more than thirty trials?"

"Yes."

"All of them for the government?"

"No. About half."

"But when you're retained, you're paid for your time?"

"Yes."

Kellogg nods, like that matters more to the jury than to him.

"You reviewed documents provided by the prosecution?"

"Yes."

"Did you review communications between the attorneys involved in preparing the filings?"

"No. I was focused on the content of the disclosures."

"So you don't know what discussions took place about those edits."

"No."

Kellogg shifts slightly, enough to suggest he's letting the jury think it through.

"Is it fair to say that you were asked to evaluate the final documents without knowing how or why they changed?"

Landon hesitates. "That's fair."

"Did you speak to anyone at the firm?"

"No."

"Did you speak to Ms. Rivers?"

"No."

"Did you speak to Mr. Carlisle, who supervised the team that submitted the disclosures?"

"No."

Kellogg pauses for effect. The jury watches Landon. He is still composed, but less comfortable.

One juror shifts forward slightly. Another scribbles something. No one looks away.

"So you formed your opinion based on the language in the filings, not the intent behind them?"

"Yes."

"Is it your role to determine intent?"

"No."

"Is it your role to suggest criminal liability?"

"No."

Kellogg steps back from the podium, hands behind his back. He's calm and steady.

"Would it surprise you to know that several partners reviewed these filings?"

"I wouldn't know that."

"Exactly."

"Would it surprise you to know that the company won the trial referenced in the filing?'

I wouldn't know that, but I believe the trial you referenced was held after the filing not before it.

He glances at the jury, then returns to his seat as if nothing more needs saying. And maybe it doesn't.

The judge turns. "Mr. Callahan, you may now cross-examine the witness."

Callahan stands and walks to the podium.

"Mr. Landon, were you asked to determine who drafted the disclosures?"

"No."

"So, you don't know whether my client, Evan Marston, contributed to or even reviewed the language in question?"

"No, I was not asked to trace authorship."

"Are you aware that Mr. Marston did not supervise the Blackwood filings?"

"I am not."

"No further questions."

Judge Dubois turns again. "Mr. Lansing, you may now cross-examine."

Lansing rises, buttoning his suit jacket.

"Mr. Landon, you testified that certain changes were material, correct?"

"Yes."

"And that they were misleading because of what was omitted?"

"Yes."

"To be clear, you're referring to final documents that included multiple levels of internal review?"

"I am referring to the final versions submitted to the SEC."

"But you don't know who approved them?"

"No."

"You don't know if Mr. Emory ever saw those drafts?"

"I do not."

"Thank you. No further questions."

After a fifteen-minute recess, we return to the courtroom. Judge Dubois glances at the government table.

"Ms. Vaughn, you may call your next witness."

Vaughn stands. "The government calls Sarah Whitcomb."

The door opens, and Sarah Whitcomb enters with the confidence of someone used to being listened to. She wears a charcoal suit, hair pulled tight, no jewelry. Everything about her is structured.

She introduces herself as the Deputy Director of Enforcement for the Securities and Exchange Commission. Vaughn walks the jury through her background. Law degree. More than fifteen years at the SEC. Lead investigator on multiple high-profile enforcement actions involving disclosure violations and misleading investor statements.

Whitcomb doesn't posture or perform.

Vaughn begins the substance of her direct.

"Ms. Whitcomb, when the SEC first began reviewing the Blackwood Holdings disclosures, what stood out to you?"

"There were key omissions in the language submitted to our office," she says. "In particular, the lack of detail around pending harassment allegations and the company's internal assessment of litigation risk."

Vaughn pulls up Exhibit 81, a timeline of the filings and internal correspondence.

Whitcomb explains that the SEC requested clarifications. She says their questions weren't answered fully or in a timely manner. She uses the phrase "pattern of minimization."

"Were these delays and omissions unusual?"

"Yes. In this context, very."

Vaughn moves to the critical point.

"In your view, did these omissions and delays materially impact the SEC's ability to evaluate the company's risk profile?"

"They did."

"Were you aware of any internal concerns raised by firm lawyers?"

"I reviewed a communication in which a junior associate raised concerns. They were not reflected in the final filings."

"Would accurate disclosures, submitted at the time, have changed your office's approach?"

"Yes. We likely would have escalated sooner and issued subpoenas earlier in the process."

Vaughn nods and returns to her table.

Judge Dubois turns toward our table. "Mr. Kellogg, you may cross-examine the witness."

Kellogg stands, unhurried.

"Ms. Whitcomb," he begins, "you're not here today because you worked directly on the Blackwood matter. Correct?"

"No. I reviewed the investigation after the fact."

"Your office received materials from the Department of Justice?"

"Yes."

"Ms. Whitcomb, the documents you reviewed came from the DOJ investigation?"

"Yes."

"You didn't gather them yourself?"

"No. They were provided to me."

"Selected by others?"

"Yes."

"Prepared by others."

"Yes."

Kellogg moves slightly, to shift the jury's focus.

"Did you ever speak with my client?"

"No."

"Anyone at her firm?"

"No."

He gives her a moment to sit in that answer before continuing.

"Yet you're offering an opinion on what the SEC would have done had different language been used in a filing?"

"Yes. Based on experience."

"Not based on personal involvement."

"No."

"Not based on actual internal communication with the firm."

"No."

Kellogg's not attacking her. He's reminding the jury that she didn't see anything. She's reading someone else's story and calling it fact.

"Ms. Whitcomb, have you ever conducted an enforcement action based solely on an inference?"

"It depends."

"That's not a yes."

"No. Not typically."

He pauses.

"And you understand that the language in these filings was reviewed by multiple people before it was submitted?"

"That is what I've been told."

"Were you also told that the Blackwood won the case referenced in the filing?"

"No, but I'm aware that the trial was held months after the filing."

He thanks her and sits. He didn't raise his voice. He didn't need to. The silence left in her answers did the work.

Judge Dubois nods. "Mr. Callahan, you may cross-examine the witness."

Callahan stands, straightens his tie.

"Ms. Whitcomb, did you ever speak with my client, Evan Marston?"

"No."

"Did you review any internal communications authored by him?"

"No."

"Are you aware of any evidence that he had direct involvement in the preparation or submission of the SEC filings?"

"No."

"That's all."

Judge Dubois turns. "Mr. Lansing?"

Lansing rises smoothly.

"Ms. Whitcomb, you testified that omissions in the filings delayed your office's response?"

"Yes."

"Do you have any evidence that my client, Blake Emory, made or approved any of those omissions?"

"No."

"Any evidence that he reviewed the final draft?"

"No."

"Thank you."

Judge Dubois looks over toward Vaughn. "Any redirect, Ms. Vaughn?"

Whitcomb steps down with the same steady posture she carried in. But something has shifted. She didn't crack, but she didn't control the room either. She followed the government's script, and Kellogg let the jury see that. His tone never changed, but every question chipped away at her certainty. Not one answer came from her own experience. Not one moment felt like it belonged to her.

I glance toward the jury box.

The older woman in the second row keeps her arms folded. She's not moved. But the young man in the back is really paying close attention now. I hold his gaze for a second too long, then look away before it becomes a moment.

Vaughn does not ask for another witness. Judge Dubois glances at the clock.

"We'll break for lunch," she says. "Back at 1:30."

I rise slowly. So does Kellogg. We walk out together, saying nothing until we're clear of the press and back in the private conference room.

"They were polished," he says finally. "But not bulletproof."

I nod. "Whitcomb didn't see anything. Landon only saw numbers."

"That's what I gave the jury."

"What about Ben?"

He doesn't answer right away. Then, "That depends on whether he's still protecting you or protecting himself."

I already know the answer.

Lunch arrives in brown bags from a place nearby. Neither of us eats much. We've got thirty minutes left, and Benjamin Carlisle is the witness Vaughn expects will sink me.

Chapter 30
The Reckoning

In boxing, you don't win just by landing punches. You win by staying on your feet when it's your turn to take them.

In law, testifying isn't about delivering a knockout. It's about standing still under pressure, answering straight, and not flinching when someone tries to make you stumble.

#

I have been waiting all morning.

The marshals keep witnesses in a small room down the hall from the courtroom. There is a table, a pitcher of water, and a stack of outdated magazines no one reads. Someone brought sandwiches at noon. I ate half of one and left the rest in the wrapper.

The government lawyers told me they would call me after lunch.

At one o'clock a clerk opens the door.

"Mr. Carlisle."

I stand and follow him down the corridor.

The courtroom is quiet when I enter. I walk past the defense tables without slowing. For a moment my eyes meet Bianca's. She smiles as if she expects me to help her.

I take the witness chair.

My right hand rests on the arm of the chair. The other lies flat in my lap while the clerk administers the oath.

Every juror is watching.

Danielle Vaughn steps to the podium.

I've been told she has prosecuted corporate fraud cases for years and rarely wastes movement. Today she carries only a yellow legal pad.

"Please state your name for the jury."

"Ben Carlisle."

"What is your profession?"

"I am a lawyer."

"How long have you practiced law?"

"A little more than twenty years."

"Where did you most recently practice?"

"At Hamilton Reed in Dallas."

"What type of work did you do there?"

"Commercial litigation and regulatory matters."

"Did that work include representing the Blackwood account?"

"Yes."

"What was your role in that representation?"

"I handled litigation strategy and defended Mr. Blackwood in the Robinson v. Blackwood trial."

A few jurors glance up at that.

"Did you also interact with Bianca Rivers in connection with that client?"

"Yes."

"In what capacity?"

"She was the partner responsible for the Los Angeles side of the account and Mr. Blackwood's primary corporate counsel."

Vaughn nods.

"During the spring before the indictments were returned, did you review proposed changes to Blackwood's SEC filings?"

"Yes."

"How did those come to your attention?"

"They were circulated internally among the partners for review."

"What was your reaction to those changes?"

"I believed they created legal exposure for both the client and the firm."

"Did you express that concern?"

"Yes."

Vaughn presses a button on the remote.

A document appears on the courtroom screen.

"Mr. Carlisle, do you recognize this memorandum dated April 14?"

"Yes. I wrote it."

"What did you say in that memorandum?"

"I wrote that there was no defensible legal rationale for the proposed adjustments and that implementing them could expose the client and the firm to enforcement risk."

"Did anyone respond to your memo?"

"Yes. I received a call from Bianca Rivers."

"What did she say?"

"She told me the issue had been handled."

"Did she explain what she meant?"

"No."

"Did you follow up?"

"Yes. I asked for written confirmation."

"Did you receive a response?"

"Yes. A short email from another partner stating the issue was understood."

"Who sent that email?"

"Eric Mendel."

"Did the conduct you warned about stop?"

"No."

"What happened instead?"

"The language changed and the timeline shifted, but the substance remained the same."

"Did you escalate your concerns?"

"Yes. I contacted the firm's general counsel."

"Did you receive a response?"

"No."

Vaughn pauses.

"Mr. Carlisle, at any point did you encourage the conduct now under investigation?"

"No."

"Did you later cooperate with the Department of Justice?"

"Yes."

"When did that occur?"

"After the indictments were unsealed."

"Why did you decide to cooperate?"

"Because the firm crossed a line and no one inside the firm stopped it."

Vaughn looks toward the judge.

"No further questions."

Judge Dubois turns to the defense table.

Mr. Kellogg stands.

He buttons his jacket before approaching the podium.

"Mr. Carlisle," he says, "you described yourself as raising concerns about the Blackwood account."

"That's correct."

"You also served as the trial lawyer who defended Mr. Blackwood in Robinson v. Blackwood?"

"Yes."

"And you won that case?"

"Yes."

"So the litigation strategy you directed resulted in a defense verdict."

"That's correct."

"And, after your success in court, you hosted a celebration in Dallas with Mr. Blackwood, Ms. Rivers, Mr. Marson, and Ms. Wolfe, isn't that true."

"Yes."

"And during the celebration of your success in court you never raised any issue about the SEC filing done before you won the case."

"No."

"You remained at Hamilton Reed throughout after that litigation, and the celebration of your success that you hosted in Dallas."

"Yes."

"After celebrating your success with them, you continued to work with the same partners you now criticize."

"I did."

"You never resigned from the firm."

"No."

"You never reported these concerns to law enforcement before the indictments."

"No."

Kellogg nods slightly.

"So, at the time all of this was happening, you continued to represent Mr. Blackwood in the Robinson case, won the case for him and then hosted Mr. Blackwood, Ms. Rivers and others for a weekend celebration of your success in Dallas."

"I did."

"And, you stayed at the firm, and continued to have interactions with Ms. Rivers."

"I stayed and raised concerns internally."

"But you stayed."

"Yes."

He lets the silence sit for a moment.

"No further questions."

Marson and Emory's lawyers simply ask if I had any interactions with their clients about the Blackwood litigation or SEC filings. I didn't so their cross examination is brief.

I am surprised when Vaughn doesn't ask me any questions on redirect.

Judge Dubois dismisses me.

I step down from the witness stand and walk past the defense table.

Bianca looks up as I pass.

She smiles again.

Outside the courtroom the hallway is warmer and quieter. A reporter near the exit raises his phone.

"Mr. Carlisle, do you believe Bianca Rivers knew it was a crime?"

I keep walking.

Two DOJ lawyers stand near the elevator. One of them nods.

"You did well," he says.

I acknowledge him and continue toward the stairwell.

Someone calls my name.

I turn.

Taylor Voss stands at the end of the hall.

"I did not expect you here," I say.

"I flew in last night," he replies. "Branson asked me to sit in."

"He's collecting opinions?"

"Something like that."

Taylor studies me for a moment.

"You looked solid in there," he says. "But people are talking."

"They always do."

"Some of them are nervous. What you said shifted things."

"That was the point."

He nods.

"You should talk to Branson. He's weighing options. People are already choosing sides."

I do not answer.

Taylor adjusts his jacket and walks down the hallway.

I wait until his footsteps fade before heading for the stairs.

Chapter 31

Bianca's Turn: The Counterpunch

In boxing, a fighter might land punches by swinging wild. But that works only until the counterpunch lands with twice the force and ends the fight.

Likewise, in law, a witness may deliver what sounds like devastating testimony. That is, until the defense lawyer dismantles him on cross-examination.

#

Los Angeles: Same Evening

I'm back at my condo after a long day in court. I'm going over what I heard today.

Ben took his swing. Some will call it measured. Others will say it was principled. But anyone who's ever watched a trial knows that it's how a witness does on cross-examination when he doesn't see what's coming.

I watched him on the stand. I waited for him to look at me. He never did, even though I kept staring at him.

I sit at the small table by the window in my condo, a glass of water beside my laptop, untouched. The lights are on. I'd normally be listening to music or watching television, but not tonight. I want it to be quiet, giving me time to think.

I heard every word Ben said. I know his tone. His pacing. The restraint behind every sentence.

Ben's not like LA lawyers. He was cautious. He outlined timelines, described standard procedures, and offered carefully worded qualifications, like to my knowledge and consistent with our role at the time. He spoke like someone trying to sound helpful without being too helpful. That may have worked when he was trying cases in Texas. But it won't work in my trial in LA.

Ben genuinely believes the truth prevails in trials. He trusts meticulous work and pristine records to protect him. Prosecutors don't deal in truth. They engineer momentum. They craft narratives, compelling stories that drag a jury, step by relentless step, toward a guilty verdict.

That will not happen to me.

My fingers tap a silent rhythm on the side of the glass. Each tap marks time, a quiet reminder to stay in control. I have spent years inside Los Angeles courtrooms.

I know how trials work here in a way Ben never will. He is used to federal court in Texas, where defendants rarely win and juries still believe that facts decide cases. Los Angeles is different. Trials here are not about absolute truths. They are about narrative, character, and how the jury feels when the story is told right.

This jury is not naive. They have seen enough to understand how the world really works. And when the case involves a celebrity they admire, they are more flexible than any jury Ben has faced in Dallas. Right now, they have not yet spotted the flaws in the government's case. But I have. And my team is ready to start pulling the threads.

I do not need the truth to win. I need the jury. And I have never lost when it mattered most.

Tomorrow, I take the stand.

****

Bianca's Turn: The Stand

Los Angeles: Wednesday Morning

The moment is here. I have spent the past two nights preparing for this. Reviewing questions with Kellogg, practicing answers, and looking in the mirror to study how I will come across. Jurors don't just listen to what you say. They watch your eyes, study your face and read the way you say it. They decide if they believe you in the first five minutes.

I wear a navy suit. No bright colors. No jewelry that might distract. I want to look professional, calm, and in control. That is what I am. I walk into the courtroom without a glance at the press row. They have written their stories already. Today, I give them something they did not expect.

Judge Dubois calls for order. The government rests. The courtroom grows still. Kellogg rises.

"The defense calls Bianca Rivers."

I walk to the witness stand and take the oath. My voice is steady. I look at the jury, not at Vaughn.

Kellogg starts with the background. My education. My rise in the firm. The Blackwood representation. I speak clearly, confidently. I know how this game is played. I have spent years preparing other witnesses. Now I am the one under the light.

I explain the firm's structure. I outline how cases are staffed, who makes final decisions, and how outside vendors are approved.

I describe my role as managing partner of the Los Angeles office. I do not dodge questions. I do not hesitate.

I tell them we represented Blackwood aggressively. We had a duty to our client. The firm never broke the law. Every case went through proper channels. Every investigation into an accuser was vetted by outside counsel or third-party investigators. I never threatened anyone. I never approved anything illegal. I gave my clients the best defense the law allowed.

Kellogg asks about the SEC filings. I state clearly that I had no role in drafting the language or reviewing the final submissions. That was handled by other lawyers. I was focused on litigation. I trusted that others were doing their jobs. If something improper happened, it did not come through me.

He moves to the accusers. Savannah Robinson. Others.

"Did you approve surveillance?"

"Yes."

I let the word sit there. I do not shrink from it.

"It was legal. Discreet. We had credible concerns about coordinated claims. Her lawyer has sued Mr. Blackwood before. We had a responsibility to understand what was behind the lawsuits. I made sure the investigations were lawful. I never ordered harassment. I never sanctioned intimidation."

Kellogg nods and moves on. He doesn't interrupt. He doesn't lead. He lets me fill the silence. Jurors listen more closely when a lawyer knows when to step back.

I talk about the hours we spent reviewing claims, trying to get to the truth. The firm's culture was one of diligence, not conspiracy. I was demanding, but I was fair. I held my team to high standards because our clients demanded nothing less.

When Kellogg finishes, I glance at the jury. No one is leaning back. They are listening.

This next part matters more than anything.

Not because I fear Vaughn. But because I know what she's going to try.

She'll paint me as ruthless, cold, and calculating. And play to the jury's distrust of lawyers.

She'll quote from emails without context and raise her voice on words like *intimidation and surveillance.*

But I didn't come here to be put down.

I came here to remind this jury that they do not have to like me to see that I'm right.

Then Vaughn stands.

She starts slowly. Asking about my title. My income. My status. She wants the jury to think I was powerful, maybe too powerful. She shifts to a tone.

"Did you call Savannah Robinson a liar in internal emails?"

"No. I said we needed to verify her story. That is not the same."

"Did you approve an investigator to follow her?"

"Yes. It was legal. Necessary."

She tries to press. She puts emails on the screen. Out of context. Stripped of nuance.

I keep calm. I explain. I do not let her rattle me.

Vaughn lifts an email and reads it like a closing argument. She's trying to build heat.

Here it is. The line they think will break me.

"You wrote: 'Make her talk or make her go away.' Those are your words, Ms. Rivers."

"Yes," I say. "And I stand by them. Because we were facing coordinated claims that could destroy a man's life. I had a duty to find out if they were real. We investigated. Legally. Quietly. Professionally."

"And Savannah Robinson? You didn't find her credible?"

"I didn't find her consistent. There's a difference."

Vaughn shifts. She tries to trap me in semantics, but I don't give her the opening.

"You surveilled her."

"No. A licensed investigator observed her. That's legal."

"You approved it."

"Absolutely. Because when someone files a multimillion-dollar lawsuit, truth becomes currency. And my job was to know what we were dealing with."

She throws Ben's testimony at me. Suggests he distanced himself because he knew something was wrong.

"Mr. Carlisle testified that you were the architect of the response strategy."

"Mr. Carlisle used the information I gave him to win the case for Blackwood. He got all the publicity from his success, but after winning and getting the publicity from his success, he now wants to judge the score."

I pause. Let that sink in.

“The truth is, we didn’t silence victims. We defended a client. We followed the law. And I refused to let a whisper campaign become a conviction.”

Vaughn frowns. The momentum has shifted.

“You’re saying you did nothing wrong.”

“I’m saying I did my job. And I won’t apologize for doing it well.”

She shifts to Ben Carlisle.

"He said you led the effort to suppress the lawsuits."

"Ben is wrong. He won the case with the help I gave him Now, he’s acting like my help was wrong.”

Vaughn frowns but moves on. She tries to imply that I micromanaged. That I knew everything. That nothing happened without me.

"You reviewed vendor invoices?"

"No. Those were handled by operations. I approved general budgets, not line items."

It goes like this for forty-five minutes. She tries to corner me. I give her no room. She wants a crack in the wall. I give her a polished stone.

When it is over, she says nothing more. No dramatic close. Just a clipped, "No further questions."

Kellogg stands again.

"One question. Ms. Rivers, did you ever intend to break the law?"

"No. I upheld it. Every single day."

I step down. I sit back beside Kellogg. The courtroom feels cooler now. The air moves again. I do not know if I changed anyone's mind. But I held the line. I told my story.

Evan Marston testifies next. He says he was not involved in the Blackwood cases that I made all major calls. That he trusted I was acting appropriately.

Then Blake Emory. His lawyer emphasizes how far removed Blake was from operational details. He blames me. Says I had control. That if something went wrong, it was on me.

I sit through it all without blinking. I expected them to try and save themselves. This is not a partnership anymore. It is survival.

Last, Kellogg calls our expert. A former federal prosecutor turned compliance consultant. He walks the jury through law firm procedures. Describes industry norms. Tells them what aggressive legal representation looks like. Tells them where the line is. Says nothing in the documents he reviewed proves we crossed it.

Then he's done. And the defense rests.

I have one chance left.

Final argument.

But that comes tomorrow.

Tonight, I breathe.

Chapter 32
The Last Word

In basketball, the first three quarters set the stage. But games are won in the fourth. When the clock is ticking and the pressure peaks, that's when the real players rise.

Trials work the same way. Facts get you to the finish. But a closing argument by a top-notch trial lawyer wins the case.

We spent yesterday afternoon arguing over jury instructions. Or at least Kellogg did. The lawyers for Evan and Blake focused on anything that might raise doubt that they were part of the scheme at all. Vaughn fought them on every word. Judge Dubois ruled with precision. A few small wins. One loss that might sting.

Kellogg didn't sugarcoat it. "We got most of what we needed," he told me outside the courtroom. "But they'll hear willful blindness, and that gives Vaughn an opening."

I nodded like it didn't bother me. But I logged it. If this jury turns, it won't be because of my story. It will be because of one phrase the judge read from the bench.

I arrive before the others because I want to control the moment. I step into the courtroom like it's mine.

The court reporter sits at her computer. The seats are already starting to fill. Reporters sit in the back row. A couple of them whisper when they see me. I don't look their way.

The jury hasn't been brought in yet, but their box is ready with clean pads, sharpened pencils, and bottled water. Every detail is in place.

I take my seat next to Kellogg. He's reviewing his outline, but when I sit down, he closes the folder.

"Vaughn will come out measured," he says. "She'll make it sound reasonable. That's the danger. She wants them to think it's common sense to convict you."

I nod. I've seen this strategy in dozens of courtrooms: build the story, make it feel inevitable, and bury the burden of proof beneath emotion.

A moment later, the courtroom doors open again. I glance back.

Ben Carlisle walks in. He looks at me, but I don't acknowledge him. He's here to see how it ends.

He takes a seat in the gallery. He's close enough to see, far enough not to be seen as part of the defense. He's allowed in now. I wonder if he'll stay through the verdict.

Then Vaughn walks in with her cadre of junior prosecutors. No folders. She and her team take their seats without a word.

I've never seen her this quiet before a hearing.

Good.

Let the jury see that.

Let them feel the shift.

Judge Dubois takes the bench a few minutes after nine. The courtroom quiets. Even the press row seems still, for once.

"Members of the jury," she begins, "thank you again for your service. We're entering the final phase of this trial."

Her voice is calm but firm. She's done this hundreds of times.

She explains the process ahead. The government will go first. Then the defense. Then the government will have a final opportunity to respond.

"After that, you will deliberate. You will first pick a foreperson. Then, you are to base your decision solely on the evidence you heard in this courtroom and the law as I instruct you," she says. "Nothing more. Nothing less."

She reminds them that the burden of proof rests entirely with the prosecution. The defendants do not have to prove anything. That if the government has failed to meet its burden, the jury must acquit.

Then she adds what every judge says and every lawyer dreads.

"You may not let sympathy, emotion, or personal feelings influence your verdict."

My eyes drift to the jury box. I look specifically at the young man who has seemingly connected with me throughout the trial. He looks back and smiles. I still think he, among others, will not vote to convict me. I just need him, and hopefully others, to hold onto those doubts a little longer.

Judge Dubois finishes her instructions. She tells Vaughn to give her the opening argument. It's showtime.

Vaughn stands slowly, like she has all the time in the world. She doesn't stride to the podium. She walks there like she's already won.

She thanks the jury for their attention. Her voice is calm, measured, with none of the sharp edges she used on cross.

"Ladies and gentlemen," she begins, "this case is about power. About what people with power do when they think no one is watching. It's about three lawyers who used their resources not just to defend their client. They used it to intimidate, silence, and conceal the victim of one of their most influential clients."

She lets that sit for a second. Then she picks up a binder.

"You heard Ms. Rivers say it herself: 'Make her talk or make her go away.' Those are not the words of someone searching for truth. They are the words of someone protecting a wealthy man who victimized a young woman. He was a wealthy, powerful man with everything to lose."

She keeps going, steady and relentless. She walks the jury through the pattern. Lawsuits filed. Private investigators deployed. Settlements quietly paid, with the occasional case pushed to trial, like the Robinson case, when the pressure failed. She emphasizes how I ran the litigation strategy, approved surveillance, and signed off on every meaningful decision.

Then she turns to the filings.

"And while Ms. Rivers was handling Blackwood's litigation," Vaughn says, "the firm was also submitting filings to the Securities and Exchange Commission. Filings that omitted material information. Filings that failed to mention the scope of legal exposure Blackwood faced. And Ms. Rivers may say she wasn't involved, but the government has shown you the timeline. The same office, the same leadership, the same concealment."

She pivots to Evan and Blake.

"This wasn't just one lawyer going too far. Mr. Marston approved litigation the litigation strategy when a case went to trial. Mr. Emory approved billing structures that kept surveillance off the books. They may claim they didn't know everything. But they knew enough."

She pauses, scans the jury.

"Willful blindness is not a defense. It's part of the crime."

She turns back to me. I sit still, composed. But I'm watching every face in that box. One juror leans forward, arms folded. Another has her lips pressed into a tight line. Most are stone-faced. Hard to read. But the young man who has connected with me is taking notes again. That's good. Note-takers want to get it right.

Vaughn wraps up by saying the case is, in the end, fairly simple. It's about what the three of us did when we thought no one would hold us accountable. She turns and points toward our table. No need to name us. The jury already knows who we are.

She says the law protects victims, but only when the truth is allowed to come forward. Mr. Blackwood was determined to keep that from happening. And we, she claims, took deliberate steps to help him do it.

Then she delivers the final hit. We didn't just try to silence accusers. We lied in the filings about Blackwood's company. We submitted false information to the Securities and Exchange Commission. That, she says, is why we're sitting at the defense table.

Then she sits down.

My turn is coming.

Judge Dubois, glances over at our table.

"Mr. Kellogg, you may address the jury."

Kellogg stands and buttons his jacket. He moves beside the podium in front of the jury with the ease of someone who's been here a thousand times. He doesn't raise his voice. He doesn't need to. He commands attention by slowing the room.

"I want to thank you for your attention," he begins. "This has been a complicated trial. You've listened carefully, and now you're being asked to do something extraordinary. You're being asked to convict people not because of what they did, but because of how it was made to sound."

He lets that settle. A pause. A measured turn toward Vaughn's table.

"This case is not about liking or disliking anyone. It's not about headlines. It's not about tactics you might not personally agree with. This is a federal criminal case. And that means proof beyond a reasonable doubt."

I watch the jurors. They're listening. I watch the young man at the end. He shifts in his seat, just slightly. It's the same look he gave me on day one, when I introduced myself with calm and confidence. I knew then he was open to my story. I know it now.

Kellogg keeps going.

"The government wants you to believe Ms. Rivers crossed a line that blurred ethics and legality. But what did she actually do? She hired licensed professional investigators to protect her client because there were real concerns about coordinated lawsuits against him, because he was a wealthy man. That's not obstruction. That's a lawyer doing what's right to protect her client from bogus lawsuits against him."

He turns back toward the jury box. "They claim she used power to intimidate. But no witness said she threatened them. Not one. Bianca Rivers gave her clients the strongest legal defense the law allowed. No document shows she ordered anything illegal. What the prosecution offered were theories and inferences, wrapped in outrage and hindsight. What they did not offer was evidence."

I glance at Vaughn. Her pen has stopped moving.

Kellogg pivots.

"And these SEC filings? Where is the email, the call, the witness who says Bianca Rivers told someone to lie? There isn't one. Because it didn't happen, she didn't draft them. She didn't edit them. She didn't see them."

His voice stays calm. Steady. Almost gentle now.

"Not liking someone's tactics is not the same as proving a crime. We cannot start locking people up for doing their jobs well. Bianca Rivers gave her clients the strongest legal defense the law allowed. That's what she was supposed to do."

He looks toward me.

"She has spent her entire career rising through the ranks, mentoring younger lawyers, protecting her clients, and building one of the most respected law offices in this city. That kind of professionalism does not disappear overnight. And it certainly doesn't turn someone into a criminal."

I catch something in the young juror's eyes. He's listening. I knew he would see through Vaughn. Kellogg is working his magic.

That's why I hired him.

Kellogg pauses once more, then finishes.

"You don't have to like everything Ms. Rivers did. You just have to ask yourself one question. Did the government prove, beyond a reasonable doubt, that she intended to break the law? If you are not convinced of that, then your duty is clear."

He nods, then sits beside me again. I keep my expression still, but inside I know what just happened.

The jury heard him.

And they heard him at his best.

The judge nods. "Mr. Leeds."

Evan's lawyer rises. He's soft-spoken. Nothing flashy. Exactly the image Evan cultivated all those years behind closed doors, never taking public credit but always pulling strings.

"Ladies and gentlemen," he begins, "my client didn't supervise the Blackwood litigation. He didn't approve of surveillance. He wasn't in the room when those decisions were made."

He keeps his tone level, almost detached, but in this case it is an unfortunate misunderstanding.

"He trusted the people around him to act appropriately. If lines were crossed, he didn't cross them. He didn't even see them."

He's distancing Evan from me. He wants the jury to think Evan was busy with other matters, too removed to be responsible for anything that happened, when in fact, Evan reviewed what I did on the Blackwood defense and approved the SEC filings.

"This isn't guilt by association," he says as he steps back from the lectern. "The government hasn't proven intent. And without that, you must return a not guilty verdict."

He sits.

Blake's lawyer, Stockton follows. He's flashier and far more dramatic. You can tell he thinks his client got dragged in by mistake.

"Mr. Emory signed off on nothing," Stockton says. "He wasn't even copied on the emails about these investigations. He's a transactional lawyer. Not a litigator. Not a manager. Not a strategist."

He points to the screen, showing a timeline stripped of anything incriminating.

"Look at the record. He's not on it. Because he wasn't involved."

I glance toward Blake. He stares straight ahead, not meeting my eyes.

I helped them build the firm. I brought in the big clients that made them wealthy. Now they act like they barely knew what we were doing.

Like it was all mine. All my calls. All my plans.

They don't say my name. But every word is a step away from me.

Stockton closes with a line that's clearly been rehearsed.

"Mr. Emory trusted his colleagues. That's not a crime. It's a risk we all take in business. And it's not enough to convict."

He sits. Neither man looks over.

I keep my expression still. But inside, I know what just happened.

My partners just let go of the rope.

Judge Dubois calls for a ten-minute recess. I walk out with Kellogg, and I tell him he made a masterful argument, and there's no way the jury can convict me now. He smiles. I'm not sure he believes me, but it doesn't matter now.

Ten minutes later, we are all back in the courtroom.

Judge Dubois stares down at Vaughn. She rises again and wastes no time. Her voice is sharper now. More direct. She walks to the center of the well and turns to face the jury.

"Do not be dazzled by lawyers wearing custom suits. The law applies the same to everyone."

She lets the sentence settle, then takes a step forward.

"When lawyers at the top review and approve, that sends a message. That's how power works. It doesn't matter if they didn't write the directive or dial the number. What matters is that nothing happened without their consent."

She paces slowly, her voice steady. "We do not need a document that says 'break the law.' We do not need a recording of a whispered order. What we have is a group of lawyers using their client's money and influence to tilt the system. They committed a crime, and they knew it. Then they knowingly lied to the Securities and Exchange Commission. It was part of a pattern. Repeated choices, made with full awareness, and executed on purpose."

She lays out the facts, but twists the narrative, ignoring the intricacies, the careful dance on the knife-edge of legality. *She calls it manipulation; I call it strategy. She'll never understand the difference.*

She gestures toward me. "Ms. Rivers wants you to believe that she was managing from a distance. That she had no idea what her firm was doing in her name. But she initiated each part of the Blackwood litigation strategy. She saw the SEC filings. This case is not about liking or disliking someone's tactics. It is about accountability."

She reminds the jury of the SEC violations. The misstatements. The filings were made under oath. She folds in Evan and Blake one last time.

"Each of these defendants made choices. They had chances to stop what was happening. They did not. And the law does not allow them to look away and walk away."

She closes her binder. "Hold them accountable."

She returns to the counsel table. Her expression is unreadable. She does not look at me.

She is overreaching. *She's trying to inflate these 'tactics' into grand conspiracies simply because she can't comprehend their sophistication*. I know it. The jury knows it.

And if they do not, they will when they start talking.

Because I gave them everything they needed to see the truth.

And I still believe they saw it.

Judge Dubois thanks the jury for their attention and reminds them of their duty. Her voice is measured, deliberate.

"You must not be influenced by sympathy, emotion, or public opinion. Your verdict must be based only on the evidence presented and the law as I give it to you."

She explains the burden of proof again. Defines reasonable doubt carefully. Then she returns to a phrase we've heard before: willful blindness.

"A defendant cannot escape responsibility by deliberately avoiding knowledge of the truth. But suspicion is not enough. You must decide whether the prosecution has proved its case beyond a reasonable doubt."

She looks toward the jury box. "You may now retire to deliberate."

One by one, they rise, including the young man I've watched from day one. He doesn't look at me. None of them do.

The door shuts behind them.

For a few seconds, the courtroom stays completely still. No one packs up. No one moves.

Kellogg exhales and leans back in his chair. I lean closer.

"What do you think?"

He doesn't answer right away. Then he straightens his cuffs and turns to me. "We gave them everything we could. If they decide on facts, you walk."

I smile. On the one hand, I'm relieved it's over. On the other hand, I'm nervous. No one can predict what a jury will do. White-collar criminal cases are rarely won by the defendants. And we're lawyers. Maybe the jurors hate lawyers. Maybe they want to send a message. I'll worry until they come back with a verdict.

But worry only gets me so far.

I told the truth. I showed them who I really am. I don't lose when it matters.

I won't lose now.

Chapter 33
Stalemate

In hockey, sometimes the game isn't settled in regulation. It drags into overtime, then a shootout, and even then, the final shot clangs off the post. The scoreboard freezes, but no one celebrates. It's not a win. It's not a loss. Just an ending with no resolution. Courtrooms can feel the same. The foreperson stands. The room holds still. But not every verdict settles the question.

#

I'm back in the courtroom to hear the verdicts. I looked over at Bianca when she walked in, but she hurried past me to her seat.

Judge Dubois looks at the foreperson.

"Have further deliberations produced any movement?"

"No, Your Honor."

"Do you believe additional deliberations would be productive?"

"No."

The judge nods once.

"As to Defendant Rivers, the court declares a mistrial."

She pauses, then continues.

"As to Defendants Marston and Emory, the jury has returned verdicts of not guilty."

Judge Dubois thanks the jury for its service and excuses them. The jurors stand and file out. No one looks toward counsel table. No one looks toward the gallery.

Not guilty for Marston. Not guilty for Emory. No verdict for her.

The reporters are already outside, grabbing sound bites. I don't give them one. I don't follow her either. There's nothing more to say.

Marston's lawyer is already at the microphone outside. Evan stands beside him, answering questions with a polished calm I've seen before. "Mr. Marston is pleased the jury saw the facts clearly," his lawyer says. "We're grateful for the outcome."

Bianca says nothing. Her lawyer issues a short statement. "We appreciate the jury's hard work. The facts are complex. If the government chooses to retry this case, we will be ready."

Bianca walks past the reporters, eyes forward. For a second, I think she might see me again. Maybe she does.

But she doesn't stop. She gets in the car without hesitation.

I don't follow. I know what she's thinking. Or I think I do.

Outside, the sky is flat gray. I see television reporters with cameras on them, but no one calls my name. A journalist near the courthouse steps asks if I'll comment. I shake my head and keep walking.

Someone I know sees me from across the plaza. Her expression freezes, then shifts before she turns away.

I don't look at my phone until I'm back at the hotel. One message from Tessa. Another from Brooke's assistant. Nothing from Bianca.

The next morning, I will catch one of the morning flights back to Dallas.

****

Bianca's Turn: Aftermath

Los Angeles: That Night

The house is quiet. The reporters are gone. So is my lawyer. I closed the blinds and turned off the ringer hours ago.

They didn't convict. That's all the jury could agree on.

There was no verdict. No closure. The jury was deadlocked, and I walked past a hallway full of cameras and kept walking.

The government will decide what to do next. They can choose a retrial, move to dismiss, or wait. But I'm not waiting for a headline to tell me who I am.

I changed out of the suit. I poured a glass of wine. I haven't touched it. I keep replaying the moment Judge Dubois said the jury was hopelessly deadlocked.

And I keep thinking about Ben.

He didn't want to testify. That much was obvious.

He didn't spin it. Didn't posture. He told what he knew and left the rest for them to decide.

People will debate whether he protected himself or sold me out. I know better.

He did what he had to do.

And in the end, it helped me more than it hurt.

I wonder if he knew that.

Suppose he could tell from where he sat that the government's story started to crack. Not all at once, but enough.

The jury didn't buy it. Not all of it.

I didn't win.

But I didn't lose either.

For tonight, that's enough.

The wine is still untouched. The room is quiet except for the occasional buzz of my phone. Messages from people I haven't heard from in months. I read none of them.

Outside, the city keeps moving. Cars pass below my window, headlights sweeping across the walls.

I don't know what comes next.

Maybe no one does.

But I'm not disappearing.

Not tonight. Not tomorrow. Not because of this.

I haven't asked what hung the jury. Not yet.

But I have a guess.

There was the young guy in the back row. He couldn't have been more than twenty-five. From the first day, he watched me more closely than anyone else. When others looked away, he kept taking notes. His focus never slipped.

By the second week, I was almost certain that he wouldn't vote to convict me.

Maybe he saw something the others missed.

Or maybe he didn't believe the government's story.

Or maybe he wasn't alone.

Or maybe he just didn't like what they were asking him to believe.

Twelve jurors with twelve versions of the truth.

And they couldn't agree on mine.

So I'll live with that.

Epilogue

Still in the Game

In boxing, sometimes the win doesn't come from a knockout. It comes from staying on your feet when the final bell rings. Taking the punches. Surviving the rounds. Staying in it until the end.

Likewise, in law, some victories aren't loud. They aren't clean. A firm might fall, but the lawyers move on. Some join other practices. Others start over with a new vision.

#

Three months later, the case is over, but not resolved. The verdict didn't come. Just a hung jury and unanswered questions. The media moved on quickly. So did most of our competitors. The old firm, the one that chased growth at any cost, no longer exists. It didn't reinvent itself. It didn't restructure. It disappeared.

Some partners lost everything they had invested. Their capital contributions evaporated in the face of contingent liabilities. The old firm signed a non-prosecution agreement and admitted it had marketed fraudulent schemes, issuing opinion letters that it knew were false. Its end wasn't sudden or dramatic. It was slow and agonizing.

But some of us never closed the door. We renegotiated our leases in Dallas and Houston.

Cassidy still works in the office next to mine. Preston's name is now on the letterhead next to mine. Locke & Carlisle is not large. But it's steady. We're no longer chasing profits per partner or trying to break into any Am Law rankings. That was the old game.

A few clients, including some of mine, stayed. Others returned when they saw we weren't going away. Some left and won't come back. We understand. Starting over means letting go.

The halls are quiet now. There are fewer people and fewer distractions, but there is more clarity. We are no longer chasing headlines or rankings. We know exactly who we are. And we remember what it cost to forget that.

Other lawyers landed in big firms. They got new titles and started over like nothing had happened. That was not our story. We stayed and rebuilt.

We were not absorbed. We did not hire a branding consultant or roll out a new image campaign.

Outside my window, Dallas keeps changing. I see cranes constructing new office buildings around me. The skyline no longer feels like a scoreboard. It's just the backdrop for a city that keeps moving, same as we do. What matters now is whether the lights come on in the morning and whether we are still here to answer when someone calls.

The work has changed. The matters we take on are simpler but more honest. The relationships are built on real conversations, not handshakes at charity events or deals struck over cocktails. Due diligence is not a checklist. It's how we operate. Every case reminds us of what we nearly lost. Every decision reflects what we have learned.

My desk is cleaner than it used to be. I keep it that way on purpose. No stacks of unsigned papers. No unanswered calls. At home, too, the noise is lower. Erin says I don't wake up in the middle of the night the way I used to. Claire is in her senior year now. She's making more NIL money than I made as a law firm associate. She's everywhere on social media. Girls in Dallas wear her number 10 jersey. At games, they line up asking for her autograph.

My attention is on the right things. Preston focuses on long-term direction. Cassidy filters everything that comes through the front door. We no longer use the word "partner" the way we once did. We are something else now. We are the ones who stayed.

One morning, Cassidy drops a folder on my desk. She does not say a word. The label on the cover is simple.

Confidential.

There is no cover letter or background memo. Only a single file, and a question no one has spoken about yet.

Cassidy stops in the doorway and finally speaks.

"They asked if you will meet next week. They are not sure they want to go forward."

I look at the folder and then back at her.

"Then we give them a reason to trust us again."

She smiles, and walks away.

I look out the window again. A Southwest Airlines plane passes by on its way to Love Field. That hasn't changed. Just a quiet reminder that life moves on.

I close the file. I sit quietly for a moment, listening to nothing in particular.

We are not chasing headlines anymore. We are not trying to be what we were.

We barely survived the onslaught. But the door stayed open.

And now, someone is knocking.

****

Bianca's Turn: Moving On

Los Angeles: Three Months Later

Three months after the mistrial, the noise has thinned. That is how I know the case has moved into its next phase. When people stop shouting, they start deciding what to do.

The Department of Justice has not announced whether it will retry the case. That silence is intentional. They want leverage without commitment. I have seen this tactic often enough to recognize it. They will wait until attention shifts and then decide whether I am worth the expense of a second attempt. I am prepared either way.

The California Bar opened an inquiry within ten days of the verdict. That was inevitable. It is administrative, not adversarial, at least for now. I produced what was requested. I answered precisely what was asked and nothing more. No findings have been issued. None may be. Bar investigations move slowly, and reputations tend to calcify long before conclusions are reached. I am not waiting on them to define me.

Blackwood is no longer a client.

That relationship ended quietly, the way most things do once the cameras are gone. There was no confrontation and no ceremony. Their board needed distance, and I had no interest in performing loyalty for people who value convenience over clarity. We concluded matters cleanly. No ongoing representation. No pending disputes. No lingering obligations. I do not miss the work.

I have not spoken to Ben Carlisle since the trial.

That is not because there is nothing to say. It is because neither of us benefits from saying it. He did what he believed was necessary. I did what I believed was required. Those truths can coexist without conversation. If we cross paths again, we will speak as professionals. If we do not, that will also be acceptable.

What has surprised some people is that I am still here.

I did not leave Los Angeles. I did not retreat into consulting or teaching or silence. I did not offer explanations or op-eds or soft-focus interviews about resilience. I returned to work. Not the same work, and not with the same visibility, but work that requires judgment, discretion, and an understanding of how institutions actually behave when they are under pressure.

Clients come differently now. They do not announce themselves. They arrive through intermediaries and old channels, through people who value outcomes over optics. They ask fewer questions, and they listen carefully to the answers. They do not ask me to promise results. They ask me whether I understand the risks. I always do.

I am aware of how I am described when my name comes up. Some people call me controlled. Others say ruthless. A few prefer calculating. None of that concerns me. Those are interpretations, not evidence. I have never needed to be liked to be effective.

The trial did not end me. It clarified me.

I know where I stand now, and I know what I am willing to defend. I am not interested in redemption arcs or public forgiveness. I am interested in leverage, precision, and timing. Those are the tools I have always relied on, and they remain intact.

The jury did not convict me. That is the only fact that matters.

Everything else is commentary.

Made in the USA
Monee, IL
12 November 2026

f0a79467-d830-4708-8177-a3c5e50a52f1R01